THE TURKEY ⎯⎯⎯⎯⎯: A
TRAVEL PREPA⎯⎯⎯ION GUIDE

SHONDA WILLIAMS

2

All rights reserved. No part of this publication may be reproduced, distributed, or transmitted in any form or by any means, including photocopying, recording, or other electronic or mechanical methods, without the prior written permission of the publisher, except in the case of brief quotations embodied in critical reviews and certain other noncommercial uses permitted by copyright law.
Copyright © (SHONDA WILLIAMS) (2023).

All images in this book are from pexels.com

Table of Contents

Introduction	**9**
Chapter 1 • Welcome to Turkey	**11**
Overview of Turkey	11
Why Visit Turkey?	14
Chapter 2 • Planning Your Trip	**19**
Best Time to Visit Turkey	19
Visa Requirements and Travel Documents	22
Airports and Airlines	26
Currency and Money Matters	29
Transportation in Turkey	32
Accommodation Options	36
Chapter 3 • Turkish Culture and Etiquette	**39**
Turkish Language and Basic Phrases	39
Cultural Norms and Customs	43
Dining Etiquette	48
Dress Code and Fashion in Turkey	51
Festivals and Celebrations	55
Chapter 4 • Exploring Turkey's Regions	**61**
Istanbul	61
Must-see Attractions in Istanbul	64
Recommendations for Accommodation	69
Recommendations for Restaurants	72
Ankara	76
Must-see Attractions in Ankara	79
Recommendations for Accommodation	81
Recommendations for Restaurants	84

Izmir	88
Must-see Attractions in Izmir	91
Recommendations for Accommodation	96
Recommendations for Restaurants	99
Bursa	103
Must-see Attractions in Bursa	105
Recommendations for Accommodation	109
Recommendations for Restaurants	112
Antalya	114
Must-see Attractions in Antalya	117
Recommendations for Accommodation	122
Recommendations for Restaurants	124
Other Turkey Regions	126
Must-see Attractions	130
Recommendations for Accommodation	133
Recommendations for Restaurants	135
Chapter 5 • Turkish Cuisine and Food Experiences	**139**
Introduction to Turkish Cuisine	139
Regional Specialties	141
Famous Turkish Dishes	145
Wine and Food Pairing	149
Culinary Experiences and Cooking Classes	152
Chapter 6 • Outdoor Activities and Nature	**155**
Hiking and Trekking in Turkey	155
Cycling in Turkey	157
Watersports inTurkey	159
Skiing in Turkey	161
Exploring National Parks	164

Beaches and Coastal Escapes 166

Chapter 7 • Shopping in Turkey 169

Fashion and Luxury Shopping 169

Local Markets and Souvenirs 171

Artisan Crafts and Workshops 173

Antique and Vintage Shopping 175

Chapter 8 • Practical Information 179

Health and Safety Tips 179

Local Laws and Customs 184

Emergency Contacts 189

Communication and Internet Access 191

Chapter 9 • Recommended Itineraries 197

Aegean Adventure Itinerary: Istanbul,   Gallipoli, Troy, Pergamum, Ephesus, Pamukkale in 7 days 197

Beaches & Ruins of the Turquoise Coast: Antalya, Kas, Kalkan, Fethiye in 7 days 202

Capitals of Empire: Istanbul, Bursa, Iznik in 7 days 207

Cappadocia Itinerary: Goreme Open Air Museum, Ihlara Valley in 2-3 days 212

Exploring the Southeast of Turkey: Mount Nemrut, Sanliurfa in 4-5 days 216

Southern Mediterranean: Side Town,   Aspendos Theatre in 7 days 221

Chapter 10 • Travelling with Children 227

Family-Friendly Attractions 227

Child-Friendly Accommodation 230

Chapter 11 • Travelling on a Budget 235

Budget-Friendly Accommodation 235

Cheap Eats and Local Food 239

Free and Affordable Attractions 243

Transportation Tips for Saving Money 247

Chapter 12 • Sustainability and Responsible Travel **253**

Sustainable Tourism in Turkey 253

Eco-Friendly Accommodation and Transportation 258

Ethical Experiences and Wildlife Conservation 262

Chapter 13 • Language and Culture Quick Reference Guide **267**

Basic Turkish Phrases and Expressions 267

Turkish Alphabet and Pronunciation Guide 276

Cultural Do's and Don'ts 282

Conclusion **287**

Introduction

Turkey is a country that defies easy categorization. It is a land of contrasts, where ancient and modern, East and West, religious and secular coexist in a dynamic and diverse mosaic. From the cosmopolitan metropolis of Istanbul, where you can marvel at the architectural wonders of the Hagia Sophia and the Blue Mosque, to the fairy-tale landscapes of Cappadocia, where you can soar in a hot-air balloon over the rock formations and cave dwellings, Turkey offers endless possibilities for exploration and discovery.

Turkey is also a country rich in history and culture, with a heritage that spans millennia and civilizations. You can walk in the footsteps of Alexander the Great, Julius Caesar, Saint Paul and Rumi, among many others, and visit the ruins of ancient cities like Troy, Ephesus and Pergamon. You can also experience the diverse traditions and cuisines of the Turkish people, who are known for their hospitality and warmth. If you are looking for adventure, relaxation, shopping or spirituality, Turkey is the right place.

In this travel guide, we will help you plan your trip to Turkey, with tips on when to go, where to go, what to do and what to expect. We will also provide you with some suggested itineraries, based on your interests and preferences. We hope you enjoy your journey to this fascinating and beautiful country.

Chapter 1 • Welcome to Turkey

Overview of Turkey

Turkey is a country that spans two continents, Europe and Asia and has a unique geographic position as a bridge and a barrier between them. Turkey has a diverse and varied landscape, with mountains, plateaus, coasts and islands. Turkey's capital is Ankara, but its largest and most famous city is Istanbul, which straddles the Bosporus strait that connects the Black Sea and the Mediterranean Sea.

Turkey has a long and rich history, dating back to ancient times when it was home to various civilizations, such as the Hittites, the Greeks, the Romans, the Byzantines, the Seljuks, the Mongols, the Ottomans and the Turks. Turkey's culture reflects this historical legacy, as well as its influences from the Middle East, the Balkans, Central Asia and Europe. Turkey's official language is Turkish, but there are also other languages spoken by ethnic minorities, such as Kurdish, Arabic, Zaza and Laz.

Turkey is the 19th-largest economy in the world, with a GDP of about US$720 billion. Turkey is a member of the OECD and the G20, and an increasingly important donor of development assistance. Turkey's economy is based on various sectors, such as industry, agriculture, tourism, services and trade. Turkey has pursued economic reforms and enjoyed high growth rates in the past two decades, but it also faces challenges such as high inflation, unemployment, poverty and external vulnerabilities.

Turkey is a country that offers many attractions and experiences for travellers, from its historical sites and natural wonders to its modern amenities and cultural festivals. Some of the best places to visit in Turkey are:

Istanbul: The former capital of the Ottoman Empire and the cultural and economic hub of Turkey. Istanbul boasts many landmarks, such as the Hagia Sophia, the Blue Mosque, the Topkapi Palace, the Grand Bazaar and the Galata Tower.

Cappadocia: A region in central Turkey that is famous for its fairy-tale scenery of rock formations, caves, valleys and hot-air balloons.

Antalya: A city on the Mediterranean coast that is a popular destination for sun-seekers and history lovers. Antalya has many beaches, resorts and ancient ruins, such as Aspendos, Perge and Termessos.

Ankara: The capital of Turkey and the second-largest city in the country. Ankara is a modern and cosmopolitan city that also has some historical attractions, such as the Anitkabir (the mausoleum of Atatürk), the Museum of Anatolian Civilizations and the Ankara Citadel.

Izmir: A city on the Aegean coast that is known for its lively atmosphere and cultural diversity. Izmir has many museums, parks, markets and festivals, as well as nearby attractions such as Ephesus (one of the best-preserved ancient cities in the world) and Pamukkale (a natural site of travertine terraces and thermal pools).

You can customise your trip to Turkey with the help of our perfectly-laid itineraries in Chapter 9, according to your budget, style and preferences.

Turkey is a country that will amaze you with its beauty, charm and diversity. Therefore, you should start planning your trip today.

Why Visit Turkey?

Turkey is a country that will captivate you with its beauty and charm. Whether you are looking for a relaxing beach holiday, a cultural adventure, a historical exploration or a natural escape, Turkey has it all. Below are some of the reasons why you should visit Turkey:

Breathtaking scenery: Turkey has a stunning and varied landscape, from the turquoise waters of the Mediterranean and Aegean seas to the fairy-tale rock formations and caves of Cappadocia, to the snow-capped mountains and lush valleys of the Black Sea and Kaçkar regions. You can enjoy the scenery by hiking, biking, paragliding, kayaking or simply admiring the views.

Fascinating history: Turkey has a rich and diverse history, dating back to ancient times when it was home to various civilizations, such as the Hittites, the Greeks, the Romans, the Byzantines, the Seljuks, the Mongols, the Ottomans and the Turks. You can see the traces of these cultures in the many archaeological sites and historical monuments that dot the country, such as Ephesus, Troy, Hagia Sophia, Topkapi Palace and Anitkabir.

Intricate architecture: Turkey's architecture reflects its historical and cultural influences, as well as its artistic and religious traditions. You can admire the majestic mosques, palaces and churches that showcase the Islamic, Byzantine and Ottoman styles, as well as the charming houses, villages and bazaars that display the local and regional characteristics. Some of the architectural highlights include the Blue Mosque, the

Grand Bazaar, the Sumela Monastery and the Safranbolu houses.

Lovely people: Turkish people are known for their friendliness, hospitality and generosity. They will welcome you with a smile, offer you tea or coffee, chat with you about their culture and life, and sometimes even invite you to their homes for dinner or to stay overnight. They will also help you with any problems or questions you may have during your trip.

The best shopping in all of Europe: Turkey is a shopper's paradise, with a variety of products to suit every taste and budget. You can find everything from carpets, ceramics, jewellery, leather goods, spices, sweets, textiles and more in the many markets, bazaars and shops that are scattered throughout the country. The Grand Bazaar in Istanbul is one of the largest and oldest covered markets in the world, with over 4,000 shops selling all kinds of goods. You can also bargain with the sellers to get the best deals.

Beautiful beaches: Turkey has a long coastline that borders three seas: the Black Sea, the Mediterranean Sea and the Aegean Sea. This means that there are plenty of beaches to choose from for sunbathing, swimming or water sports. Some of the best beaches include

Oludeniz's Blue Lagoon (where you can also paraglide over it), Antalya's Kaputas Beach (nestled between two cliffs), Izmir's Cesme Beach (popular for windsurfing) and Bodrum's Gumbet Beach (known for its nightlife).

Turkish baths: One of the most relaxing and enjoyable experiences in Turkey is to visit a Turkish bath or hammam. This is a traditional ritual that involves cleansing and pampering your body in a steamy room with marble slabs and basins. You can get scrubbed by an attendant or do it yourself with a case (a rough cloth) and soap. You can also get a massage or an oil treatment to complete your spa session.

Archaeological sites: Turkey has some of the most impressive and well-preserved archaeological sites in the world. You can see ancient cities that were once thriving centres of civilization, such as Ephesus (one of the seven wonders of the ancient world), Troy (the legendary site of the Trojan War), Pergamon (a UNESCO World Heritage Site) and Hierapolis (a spa town with thermal pools). You can also see underground cities that were built by early Christians to escape persecution, such as Derinkuyu and Kaymakli in Cappadocia.

Excellent museums: Turkey also has some of the best museums that showcase its rich cultural heritage and artistic achievements. You can see priceless artefacts from different periods and regions in museums such as the Museum of Anatolian Civilizations in Ankara (which won the European Museum of the Year Award in 1997), the Istanbul Archaeological Museums (which house over one million objects), the Zeugma Mosaic Museum in Gaziantep (which is the largest mosaic museum in the world) and the Mevlana Museum in Konya (which is dedicated to Rumi, a famous poet and mystic).

Start planning your trip today!

Chapter 2 • Planning Your Trip

Best Time to Visit Turkey

Turkey is a country that can be enjoyed all year round, depending on your preferences and interests. However, some months are more suitable than others for certain activities and destinations. Below is a month-by-month breakdown of the best time to visit Turkey:

January and February: These are the coldest and windiest months in Turkey, especially in Istanbul and the inland regions. However, this also means fewer crowds and lower prices for accommodation and flights. You can visit the museums and historical sites without long queues, or enjoy the winter scenery of Cappadocia with snow-capped fairy chimneys. You can also ski in some of the mountain resorts, such as Uludag or Palandoken.

March and April: These are the months when spring arrives in Turkey, bringing warmer temperatures and blooming flowers. This is a great time to visit the Aegean and Mediterranean coasts, where you can enjoy the beaches and ancient ruins without the summer heat and crowds. You can also witness the spectacular tulip festival in Istanbul, where millions of tulips are planted in parks and gardens across the city.

May and June: These are the months when summer begins in Turkey, with sunny days and pleasant nights. This is a popular time to visit Turkey, especially for beach lovers and outdoor enthusiasts. You can swim, sunbathe, snorkel or dive along the Turquoise Coast, or hike, bike, paraglide or kayak in Cappadocia, Pamukkale or the Black Sea mountains. You can also join some of the lively festivals and events that take place in Istanbul and other big cities.

July and August: These are the hottest and busiest months in Turkey, with temperatures reaching up to 40°C (104°F) in some places. This is the peak season for tourism, so expect higher prices and larger crowds everywhere. However, this is also the best time to enjoy the vibrant nightlife and entertainment options in Turkey, from beach parties to cultural shows. You can also cool off in some of the natural pools or waterfalls that are scattered throughout the country.

September and October: These are the months when autumn sets in Turkey, bringing cooler temperatures and colourful foliage. This is another ideal time to visit Turkey, as you can still enjoy the beaches and outdoor activities without the summer crowds and heat. You can also experience some of the local harvest festivals that celebrate the fruits of the season, such as grapes, olives, artichokes or apricots.

November and December: These are the months when winter returns to Turkey, bringing colder temperatures and possible rain or snow. This is a low season for tourism, so you can find good deals and fewer visitors in most places. You can visit the museums and historical sites with more comfort and ease, or relax in a Turkish bath or a cosy tavern. You can also celebrate

Christmas or New Year's Eve in Turkey, with festive decorations and events.

Visa Requirements and Travel Documents

If you are planning to visit Turkey, you may need to obtain a visa depending on your nationality and the purpose of your trip. Turkey offers different types of visas, such as e-Visa, sticker visas and visas on arrival. You can check the visa regime for your country on the website of the Ministry of Foreign Affairs of Turkey.

One of the most convenient and popular ways to get a visa for Turkey is to apply for an e-Visa online. This is an

22

electronic authorization that allows you to enter and travel within Turkey for tourism or business purposes. You can apply for an e-Visa on the official website of the Republic of Turkey in three easy steps:

- Fill in the online application form with your personal and travel information
- Pay the visa fee with a credit or debit card
- Download and print your e-Visa

To be eligible for an e-Visa, you must meet the following requirements:

- Hold a valid passport that has at least six months of validity from the date of your arrival in Turkey
- Have proof of sufficient income or funds to cover your expenses during your stay
- Have proof of round-trip flight tickets and hotel reservations
- Hold all the documents that are required for your destination country
- Meet all the criteria mentioned on the e-Visa order form

Please note that an e-Visa is only valid for tourism or business purposes. For other purposes, such as work, study or residence, you need to apply for a sticker visa at the nearest Turkish embassy or consulate.

A sticker visa is a physical visa that is affixed to your passport. You need to apply for a sticker visa in person or through an authorized agent at the nearest Turkish diplomatic mission. You need to submit the following documents along with your visa application form:

- A valid passport that has at least six months of validity from the date of your departure from Turkey
- Two recent passport-sized photos that meet the photo requirements
- A letter of invitation or sponsorship from a person or organization in Turkey, if applicable
- A letter of employment or enrollment from your employer or school, if applicable
- A travel insurance policy that covers your medical expenses in Turkey, if applicable
- A bank statement or other proof of financial means to cover your expenses during your stay
- A visa fee payment receipt

The processing time and fee for a sticker visa may vary depending on your nationality, type of visa and duration of stay. You can check the visa fees for your country on the website of the Ministry of Foreign Affairs of Turkey.

Some countries are also eligible for a visa on arrival, which is a visa that you can obtain at the port of entry in Turkey. However, this option is not recommended as it may involve long queues and higher fees. It is advisable to apply for an e-Visa or a sticker visa in advance to avoid any inconvenience.

Regardless of the type of visa you have, you need to register yourself at the nearest local police department within 30 days of your arrival in Turkey, if you intend to stay longer than 90 days. You also need to have a travel document or passport valid for at least six months from the date of your arrival in Turkey.

Airports and Airlines

Turkey is a popular destination for travellers from all over the world, thanks to its rich culture, history, cuisine and natural beauty. If you are planning to visit Turkey, you will need to know some basic information about its airports and airlines.

Airports in Turkey

Turkey has 51 airports with scheduled flights, serving both domestic and international destinations. The largest and busiest airport in Turkey is **Istanbul Airport (IST)**, which opened in 2018 and replaced the former Atatürk International Airport as the main hub for Turkish Airlines. Istanbul Airport is located about 40 km northwest of the city centre and has flights to 307 destinations in 116 countries. It is one of the biggest airports in the world, with a capacity of 200 million passengers per year.

Another major airport in Istanbul is **Sabiha Gökçen International Airport (SAW)**, which is located on the Asian side of the city and serves mainly low-cost carriers. Sabiha Gökçen has flights to 98 destinations in 35 countries and is the second busiest airport in Turkey.

Other important airports in Turkey include:

Antalya Airport (AYT): The main gateway to the Mediterranean coast of Turkey, Antalya Airport has flights to 63 destinations in 28 countries, mostly seasonal charter flights from Europe. It is the third busiest airport in Turkey and the ninth busiest in Europe.

Ankara Esenboğa Airport (ESB): The capital city of Turkey, Ankara, is served by Esenboğa Airport, which has flights to 43 destinations in 10 countries. It is the fourth busiest airport in Turkey and the 13th busiest in Europe.

İzmir Adnan Menderes Airport (ADB): The largest city on the Aegean coast of Turkey, İzmir, is served by Adnan Menderes Airport, which has flights to 44 destinations in 12 countries. It is the fifth busiest airport in Turkey and the 14th busiest in Europe.

Airlines in Turkey

The flag carrier and largest airline in Turkey is **Turkish Airlines**, which is also one of the largest airlines in the world. Turkish Airlines flies to 331 destinations in 127 countries, covering all continents except Antarctica. It has a fleet of 407 aircrafts, ranging from narrow-body jets to wide-body jets and cargo planes. Turkish Airlines is a member of Star Alliance and has codeshare agreements with many other airlines.

Other major airlines based in Turkey include:

Pegasus Airlines: A low-cost carrier that flies to 120 destinations in 42 countries, mostly in Europe, Asia and Africa. It has a fleet of 95 aircrafts, all narrow-body jets. Pegasus Airlines is not a member of any airline alliance but has codeshare agreements with some airlines.

SunExpress: A joint venture between Turkish Airlines and Lufthansa, SunExpress flies to 66 destinations in 20 countries, mainly in Europe, Asia and Africa. It has a fleet of 53 aircrafts, all narrow-body jets. SunExpress is not a member of any airline alliance but has codeshare agreements with some airlines.

Corendon Airlines: A leisure airline that flies to 145 destinations in 45 countries, mostly seasonal charter flights from Europe. It has a fleet of 29 aircrafts, all narrow-body jets. Corendon Airlines is not a member of any airline alliance but has codeshare agreements with some airlines.

We hope this section helps you plan your trip to Turkey. Have a safe and enjoyable flight!

Currency and Money Matters

Turkey is a country with a rich culture, history and natural beauty. If you are visiting Turkey, you will need to know some basic information about its currency and other money matters.

Currency in Turkey

The official currency of Turkey is the Turkish lira (TRY), which is also used in the Turkish Republic of Northern Cyprus. The Turkish lira has a unique symbol (₺) that was introduced by the Turkish Central Bank in 2012. The Turkish lira is divided into 100 kuruş (Kr), and there are coins of 1, 5, 10, 25 and 50 kuruş, and 1 lira. There are also banknotes of 5, 10, 20, 50, 100 and 200 lines. All the coins and banknotes have images of Mustafa Kemal Atatürk, the founder of modern Turkey.

The Turkish lira is the best currency to use in Turkey, as it is the only legal tender accepted everywhere. Some tourist areas may accept other currencies, such as euros or U.S. dollars, but the rates will not be favourable and you may not get change in the same currency. It is advisable to use Turkish liras for all your transactions in Turkey.

Money Matters in Turkey

There are several ways to obtain Turkish liras in Turkey. The easiest and cheapest way is to use your debit or credit card at an ATM (cash machine). You can find ATMs in most cities and towns, as well as airports, hotels and shopping malls. However, you should check with your bank before you travel about the fees and limits for using your card abroad. You should also inform your bank that you are travelling to Turkey to avoid any problems with your card being blocked.

Another option is to exchange your foreign currency at a currency exchange office. You can find these offices in most tourist areas, especially near the Grand Bazaar in Istanbul, where the competition drives a good deal for travellers. You should avoid exchanging your money at airports or hotels, as they usually offer worse rates than in city centres. You may need to show your passport and provide some details when exchanging your money at an office.

You can also use your debit or credit card to pay for some goods and services in Turkey, such as hotel rooms, car rentals or online purchases. However, you should be aware that some places may not accept cards or may charge extra fees for using them. You should also check the exchange rate that is applied by the merchant or your bank before you pay with your card.

Traveller's checks are not recommended in Turkey, as they are a hassle to use and may not be accepted by many places. You may also have to pay high fees to cash them at banks or exchange offices.

When paying with cash in Turkey, it is good to have some smaller notes and coins with you, as many people may not accept large notes for small payments or may not have enough change. You should also check your change carefully and keep your receipts for any purchases.

We hope this section helps you prepare for your trip to Turkey. Have a wonderful time!

Transportation in Turkey

Turkey is a large and diverse country that offers many attractions for travellers. To explore its cities, coasts and mountains, you will need to know basic information about its transportation options.

Turkey has a well-developed and affordable public transport system that covers most of the country. You can choose from various modes of transportation, such as planes, buses, trains, minibuses, ferries and subways, depending on your destination, budget and preference.

Planes: Turkey has nearly 50 airports that serve domestic and international flights. Flying is the fastest and most convenient way to travel between major cities and regions, especially if you book in advance or find a cheap deal. The main airlines are Turkish Airlines, Pegasus Airlines, SunExpress and AnadoluJet. You can find bus or taxi transfers from the airports to the city centres or nearby towns.

Buses: Buses are the most common and popular way to travel around Turkey, as they are frequent, comfortable and relatively cheap. You can find buses of different sizes and standards that connect all the cities and towns in Turkey, as well as some neighbouring countries. Most long-distance buses have reclining seats, snack service, wi-fi and entertainment systems. They also stop at rest areas every few hours for passengers to eat, smoke, pray or shop. You can buy bus tickets online or at the bus stations (otogar). Some of the major bus companies are Kamil Koç, Pamukkale and Varan.

Trains: Trains are not very widely used in Turkey, as they are slow, infrequent and limited in routes. However, they are scenic, relaxing and sometimes cheaper than buses or planes. The train network is run by Turkish State Railways (TCDD), which is undergoing a major overhaul to introduce new high-speed lines between Ankara and Istanbul, Konya and Sivas. You can check the train schedules and buy tickets online or at the train stations.

Minibuses: Minibuses are small vans or buses that run on fixed routes within or between cities and towns. They are also known as dolmuş (meaning "filled") or minibüs. They are cheap, fast and flexible, as they depart when they are full of passengers and stop anywhere on request. You can find minibuses at the bus stations or on the main streets. You have to tell the driver where you want to get off and pay the fare when you exit.

Ferries: Ferries are a great way to travel across the seas and lakes in Turkey, as well as to some of the islands and neighbouring countries. They are scenic, comfortable and sometimes faster than road transport. You can find ferries of different sizes and standards that operate on regular schedules or demand. You can buy ferry tickets online or at the ports. Some of the main ferry operators are İDO, BUDO and Turyol.

Subways: Subways are available in some of the major cities in Turkey, such as Istanbul, Ankara, Izmir and Bursa. They are fast, modern and convenient for avoiding traffic jams and reaching the city centres or attractions. You can buy subway tickets or cards at the stations or kiosks. You can check the subway maps and timetables online or at the stations.

You can also use other modes of transportation in Turkey, such as taxis, car rentals, bicycles or motorcycles. However, you should be aware of the traffic rules, safety issues and costs involved in using them.

We hope this section helps you plan your trip to Turkey. Have a fun and safe journey!

Accommodation Options

Turkey is a country that offers a variety of accommodation options for travellers of different tastes, budgets and needs. You can find hotels, guesthouses, apartments, hostels, campsites and more in Turkey, depending on where you want to stay and what you want to experience.

Hotels: Hotels are the most common and popular type of accommodation in Turkey, especially in the major cities, tourist areas and coastal resorts. You can find hotels of different sizes, standards and prices, from luxury five-star hotels to budget-friendly two-star hotels. Most hotels offer amenities such as private bathrooms, air conditioning, wi-fi, TV, minibar and breakfast. Some hotels also have facilities such as restaurants, bars, pools, spas and gyms. You can book hotels online or at the reception.

Guesthouses: Guesthouses are also known as pensions or butik hotels in Turkey. They are usually family-run establishments that offer simple but cosy rooms with shared or private bathrooms. They are cheaper than hotels and often include breakfast and sometimes dinner. They are a great way to experience the local hospitality and culture, as well as to meet other travellers. You can find guesthouses in most towns and villages, especially in the western and southern regions. You can book guesthouses online or by phone.

Apartments: Apartments are self-catering units that offer more space, privacy and flexibility than hotels or guesthouses. They usually have one or more bedrooms, a living room, a kitchen and a bathroom. They are ideal for families, groups or long-term stays. They are more common in big cities and tourist areas, where you can find them in different locations, sizes and prices. You can book apartments online or by phone.

Hostels: Hostels are budget-friendly accommodation options that offer dormitory-style rooms with bunk beds and shared bathrooms. They are popular among backpackers, solo travellers and young people who want to socialize and save money. They usually have common areas such as lounges, kitchens and laundry facilities. Some hostels also offer private rooms for more comfort and privacy. You can find hostels in most of the big cities and tourist areas, especially in Istanbul, Ankara, Izmir and Cappadocia. You can book hostels online or at the reception.

Campsites: Campsites are outdoor accommodation options that offer pitches for tents, caravans or motorhomes. They are cheap, natural and adventurous ways to stay in Turkey, especially if you want to explore its rural areas and national parks. They usually have basic facilities such as toilets, showers, electricity and water. Some campsites also have amenities such as restaurants, shops, pools and playgrounds. You can find campsites in many regions of Turkey, especially along the Aegean and Mediterranean coasts. You can book campsites online or by phone.

We hope this section helps you choose your accommodation option in Turkey. Have a pleasant stay!

Chapter 3 • Turkish Culture and Etiquette

Turkish Language and Basic Phrases

If you are visiting Turkey, you will need to know some basic information about its language and some useful phrases to communicate with the locals.

Turkish is the official language of Turkey, spoken by about 80 million people in the country and around the world. Turkish belongs to the Turkic language family, which includes languages such as Azerbaijani, Kazakh and Uzbek. Turkish is written in the Latin alphabet but with some additional letters such as ç, ğ, ı, ö, ş and ü. Turkish is an agglutinative language, which means that it forms words by adding suffixes to the roots. For example, the word ev means "house" and the suffix -de means "in", so evde means "in the house". Turkish also has two grammatical genders (masculine and feminine), two numbers (singular and plural) and six cases (nominative, accusative, dative, genitive, ablative and locative). Turkish word order is usually subject-object-verb (SOV), which means that the verb comes at the end of the sentence. For example, Ben kitap okuyorum means "I am reading a book" (literally "I book read"). Turkish pronunciation is mostly phonetic, which means that each letter has a fixed sound and there are few exceptions. However, some sounds may be difficult for English speakers to produce or distinguish, such as the soft g (ğ), the dotted i (ı) or the undotted i (i).

Basic Phrases

Learning some basic phrases in Turkish can help you communicate with the locals, express your needs and wishes, and show your respect and appreciation for their culture. Below are some of the most common and useful phrases in Turkish for tourists:

Hello / Hi: Merhaba / Selam (mare-aba / salam)

Good morning / Good day / Good evening / Good night: Günaydın / İyi günler / İyi akşamlar / İyi geceler (goon-eye-din / ee-goon-lair / ee-ak-shahm-lar / ee-geh-jeh-lar)

How are you?: Nasılsın? (na-suhl-suhn)

I'm fine, thank you: İyiyim, teşekkürler (ee-yee-yim, teh-sheh-kewr-ler)

What's your name?: Adın ne? (informal) / Adınız ne? (formal) (a-duhn neh / a-duh-nuhz neh)

My name is ...: Benim adım ... (beh-nim a-duhm ...)

Nice to meet you: Memnun oldum (mem-nun ol-dum)

Thank you / You're welcome: Teşekkürler / Bir şey değil (teh-sheh-kewr-ler / beer shey dey-eel)

Excuse me / I'm sorry: Pardon / Özür dilerim (par-don / er-zewr di-leh-rim)

Yes / No: Evet / Hayır (eh-vet / high-uhr)

Please: Lütfen (lew-tfen)

Do you speak English?: İngilizce konuşuyor musun? (informal) / İngilizce konuşuyor musunuz? (formal) (ing-gi-liz-jeh ko-noo-shoo-yor moo-sun / moo-suh-nuz)

I don't understand: Anlamadım (an-la-ma-duhm)

Can you help me?: Bana yardım edebilir misin? (informal) / Bana yardım edebilir misiniz? (formal) (ba-na yar-duhm eh-deh-bi-leer mee-sin / mee-suh-nuz)

Where is ...?: ... nerede? (... neh-reh-deh)

How much is ...?: ... ne kadar? (... neh ka-dar)

Do you have ...?: ... var mı? (... var muh)

I want ...: ... istiyorum (... is-tee-yo-rum)

I like ...: ... seviyorum (... seh-vee-yo-rum)

I don't like ...: ... sevmiyorum (... seh-vee-yo-rum)

Cheers!: Şerefe! (sheh-reh-feh)

Goodbye: Hoşçakal (informal) / Güle güle (formal) (hosh-cha-kal / gew-leh gew-leh)

We hope this section helps you learn some Turkish language and basic phrases. Have a nice trip!

Cultural Norms and Customs

If you are visiting Turkey, you will need to know some basic information about its cultural norms and customs, which may differ from your own.

Turkey is a secular republic with a predominantly Muslim population. However, Turkish culture is also influenced by its Anatolian, Ottoman, European and Middle Eastern heritage. Therefore, you may encounter a variety of customs and traditions in different regions, communities and occasions. Below are some of the most common and important ones to be aware of:

Greetings: Turks greet each other by kissing both cheeks, starting from the right. This is done between people of the same gender or between women and men who are relatives or close friends. Otherwise, a handshake is more appropriate. Turks also use verbal greetings such as merhaba (hello), günaydın (good morning), iyi günler (good day), iyi akşamlar (good evening) and iyi geceler (good night). When addressing someone older or more senior than you, it is polite to use their title (such as bey for Mr., hanım for Mrs., and Doktor for doctor) followed by their first name.

Eye contact: Turks maintain eye contact when speaking to show interest and sincerity. However, prolonged or direct eye contact may be considered rude or aggressive, especially between men. It is also disrespectful to stare at someone of the opposite sex or someone who is older or more senior than you.

Personal space: Turks tend to stand closer than Westerners when conversing or queuing. This does not imply intimacy or aggression, but rather friendliness and warmth. However, physical contact between people of the opposite sex who are not related or close friends is generally avoided in public, especially in conservative areas.

Body language: Turks use a lot of gestures and facial expressions when communicating. Some of them may be different from what you are used to. For example, nodding your head up and back while making a clicking sound with your tongue means "no" or "there isn't any". Shaking your head from side to side while making a tsk sound means "I don't know" or "I don't care". Raising your eyebrows and chin while inhaling sharply means "I'm surprised" or "Really?". Pointing your index finger to your temple means "you're smart" or "that's a good idea". Holding your hand up with your palm facing out and wiggling your fingers means "Come here" or "Hurry up". However, some gestures may be considered rude or offensive, such as pointing at someone with your finger, showing the soles of your feet or shoes, crossing your legs when sitting in front of an elder or a superior, or making the OK sign with your thumb and index finger.

Hospitality: Turks are very hospitable and generous to their guests. If you are invited to someone's home, it is customary to bring a small gift such as flowers, chocolates, sweets or fruit. You should also remove your shoes at the door and compliment the host on their house. You will be offered tea, coffee or other refreshments, which you should accept unless you have a valid reason not to. You may also be served a full meal, which you should decline at first but accept after being insisted upon. You should eat everything on your plate and praise the food. You should not leave immediately after finishing your meal, but stay for some conversation and more tea or coffee.

Religion: Turkey is a secular state that guarantees freedom of religion for its citizens. However, most Turks are Muslims who follow the Sunni branch of Islam. Islam has five pillars: shahada (declaration of faith), salat (prayer), zakat (charity), sawm (fasting) and hajj (pilgrimage). Muslims pray five times a day facing Mecca, the holiest city in Islam. The call to prayer (ezan) can be heard from mosques throughout the country. The most important religious festival in Turkey is Ramadan (Ramazan), the ninth month of the Islamic calendar when Muslims fast from dawn to dusk. Another important festival is Eid al-Adha (Kurban Bayramı), which commemorates the willingness of Abraham to sacrifice his son Ishmael. On this occasion, Muslims slaughter an animal (usually a sheep or a goat) and distribute its meat to the poor.

Dress code: Turkey is a modern and diverse country where people dress according to their personal style, profession and location. However, some general rules apply, especially for foreigners who want to avoid unwanted attention or disrespect. In urban areas, Western-style clothing is common and acceptable, but revealing or tight-fitting outfits should be avoided. In rural areas, conservative and modest clothing is preferred, such as long skirts or trousers, long-sleeved shirts or blouses, and scarves or hats for women. In religious or historical sites, such as mosques or museums, visitors should cover their shoulders, knees and heads (for women). Shoes should also be removed before entering a mosque. Nude or topless sunbathing is not allowed anywhere in Turkey.

We hope this section helps you understand and respect the cultural norms and customs in Turkey. Have a wonderful time!

Dining Etiquette

If you are visiting Turkey, you will need to know some basic information about its dining etiquette, which may differ from your own.

Turks love food and enjoy sharing it with their guests. Dining in Turkey can be a social and cultural experience, as well as a gastronomic one. Below are some of the most common and important rules to follow when dining in Turkey:

Greetings: When you enter a restaurant or someone's home, you should greet the staff or the host with a smile and a verbal greeting such as merhaba (hello), günaydın (good morning), iyi günler (good day) or iyi akşamlar (good evening). You should also say afiyet olsun (enjoy your meal) before you start eating or when you serve someone else. The appropriate response is teşekkürler (thank you) or sağol (thanks).

Seating: In restaurants, you can usually choose your table, unless there is a sign that says rezervasyonlu (reserved). In someone's home, you should wait for the host to show you where to sit. The honoured guest usually sits next to the host or on the side of the table farthest from the door. Men and women may sit separately or together, depending on the occasion and the preference of the host.

Ordering: In restaurants, you will be given a menu (menü) and sometimes a specials board (günlük yemek). You can ask for recommendations (tavsiye) from the waiter (garson) or the owner (sahip). You can also ask for the price (fiyat) of any dish before ordering. You should order one main dish (ana yemek) per person, and optionally some appetizers (meze), salads (salata), soups (çorba), bread (ekmek) and drinks (içecek). You can order water (su), tea (çay), coffee (kahve), juice (meyve suyu), soda (gazoz), beer (bira), wine (şarap) or raki (an anise-flavoured alcoholic drink). You should specify if you want your drink cold (soğuk) or hot (sıcak), with or without sugar (şekerli or şekersiz), with or without ice (buzlu or buzusuz), with or without milk (sütlü or sütsüz).

Eating: Turks eat with forks, spoons and knives, Western style. The fork is held in the left hand and the knife in the right hand. Do not switch hands for knives and forks. You can also use bread to scoop up food from your plate or a communal dish. You should use your right hand for eating, as the left hand is considered unclean. You should eat everything on your plate, as leaving food may be seen as wasteful or disrespectful. You should also try everything that is offered to you unless you have dietary restrictions or allergies. You can indicate that you are finished by placing your knife and fork side by side on your plate.

Paying: In restaurants, you can ask for the bill (hesap) by making eye contact with the waiter and holding up your hand. You can pay by cash (nakit) or credit card (kredi kartı). Tipping is not mandatory but appreciated. A tip of 10% to 15% of the bill is considered generous. You can leave the tip on the table or add it to the bill if paying by card. In someone's home, you should not offer to pay for anything, as this may be seen as rude or insulting. Instead, you should thank the host for their hospitality and compliment them on their food.

Leaving: When you leave a restaurant or someone's home, you should say goodbye (hoşçakal or güle güle) and wish them well. You can also say elinize sağlık (health to your hands) to the cook to show your appreciation for their food.

We hope this section helps you enjoy your dining experience in Turkey. Afiyet olsun!

Dress Code and Fashion in Turkey

Turkey is a country with a modern and diverse fashion scene, influenced by its Anatolian, Ottoman, European and Middle Eastern heritage. If you are visiting Turkey, you will need to know some basic information about its dress code and fashion, which may vary depending on where you are and what you are doing.

Turkey is a secular state that guarantees freedom of expression for its citizens. However, most Turks are Muslims who follow the Sunni branch of Islam. Therefore, you may encounter different levels of conservatism and modesty in different regions, communities and occasions. Below are some of the general guidelines to follow when dressing in Turkey:

In urban areas: In big cities like Istanbul, Ankara, Izmir or Antalya, you can wear pretty much what you want, as long as it is not too revealing or offensive. Western-style clothing is common and acceptable, such as jeans, T-shirts, skirts, dresses, shorts, etc. You can also express your style with accessories, colours, patterns and trends. However, you should avoid wearing clothes that are too tight, too short or too low-cut, especially in conservative neighbourhoods or religious sites. You should also respect the local culture and customs by covering your shoulders, knees and head (for women) when visiting mosques or other sacred places.

In rural areas: In small towns and villages, especially in the eastern and southeastern regions of Turkey, you should dress more conservatively and modestly than in urban areas. You should avoid wearing clothes that expose too much skin or attract too much attention. You should opt for long skirts or trousers, long-sleeved shirts or blouses, and scarves or hats for women. Men should also wear long trousers, shirts with long sleeves, and shoes that cover the ankles. You should also be prepared to cover your head (for women) or remove your shoes when entering someone's home or a mosque.

In coastal areas: In coastal resort areas of Turkey, such as Bodrum, Marmaris or Fethiye, you can wear more casual and relaxed clothing than in other parts of the country. You can wear shorts, T-shirts, tank tops, bikinis, flip-flops, etc., as long as they are appropriate for the beach or the pool. However, you should not wear beachwear outside of these areas, such as in restaurants, shops or streets. You should also bring a nice dress or a jacket for dinner at a fancy hotel or restaurant. You should also wear flat shoes instead of heels because many summer venues are located by or on the beach.

In winter: In winter (December), you will need warm woollen clothing and rain gear for most parts of Turkey, especially in the northern and central regions. You will need coats, jackets, sweaters, scarves, gloves and boots to keep yourself warm and dry. You may also encounter snow in some places like Ankara or Erzurum. However, some parts of Turkey may still have mild weather in winter, such as the Mediterranean coast or the southeast. In these areas, you may only need a light jacket or a sweater for cool evenings.

We hope this section helps you choose what to wear in Turkey. Have a great time!

Festivals and Celebrations

If you are visiting Turkey, you will need to know some basic information about its festivals and celebrations, which reflect its Anatolian, Ottoman, European and Middle Eastern heritage.

Turkey has more than 1000 festivals that are held throughout the year in almost every city of the country. Some of these festivals are of local scale, while others are of international reach and attract visitors from all over the world. Some of these festivals are based on religious, national or historical occasions, while others are based on artistic, musical or cultural themes. Below are some of the most popular and important festivals and celebrations in Turkey:

National Holidays: Turkey has six national holidays that commemorate significant events in its history and honour its founder, Mustafa Kemal Atatürk. These holidays are:

April 23rd: National Sovereignty and Children's Day. This holiday celebrates the establishment of the Grand National Assembly in 1920, which marked the start of the Turkish War of Independence. It also dedicates the day to children as the future of the nation. On this day, children from different countries perform shows in traditional costumes, while local children participate in various activities and events.

May 19th: Commemoration of Atatürk, Youth and Sports Day. This holiday celebrates the birthday of Atatürk and his landing at Samsun in 1919, which ignited the Turkish War of Independence. It also honours the youth as the heirs of the republic. On this day, young people perform sports competitions, parades and ceremonies, while famous musicians give free concerts.

August 30th: Victory Day. This holiday celebrates the decisive victory of the Turkish army over the invading

Greek forces at the Battle of Dumlupınar in 1922, which ended the Turkish War of Independence. On this day, military parades, ceremonies and fireworks take place across the country.

October 29th: Republic Day. This holiday celebrates the proclamation of the Turkish Republic in 1923 by Atatürk. On this day, official ceremonies, speeches and performances take place, while people decorate their homes and streets with flags and images of Atatürk.

November 10th: Atatürk Memorial Day. This holiday commemorates the death anniversary of Atatürk in 1938. On this day, people pay tribute to his legacy by visiting his mausoleum in Ankara or laying wreaths at his statues. At 09:05 am, the exact time of his death, sirens sound and people observe a minute of silence.

January 1st: New Year's Day. This holiday marks the beginning of the new year according to the Gregorian calendar. On this day, people exchange gifts, make resolutions and celebrate with parties, fireworks and music.

Religious Holidays: Turkey is a secular state that guarantees freedom of religion for its citizens. However, most Turks are Muslims who follow the Sunni branch of Islam. Therefore, they observe two major religious holidays that follow the lunar calendar and fall 11 days earlier each year. These holidays are:

Ramadan (Ramazan). This is the ninth month of the Islamic calendar when Muslims fast from dawn to dusk and abstain from worldly pleasures. It is a time of spiritual reflection, charity and self-discipline. During Ramadan, mosques are beautifully illuminated and recite verses from the Quran. People break their fast at sunset with a meal called iftar, which they often share with family and friends. They also attend special prayers called tarawih at night. The end of Ramadan is marked by a three-day festival called Eid al-Fitr (Şeker Bayramı), which means "Festival of Breaking the Fast" or "Sugar Festival". On this occasion, people dress in new clothes, visit their relatives and neighbours, exchange gifts and sweets, and give alms to the poor.

Eid al-Adha (Kurban Bayramı). This is another three-day festival that takes place about two months after Ramadan. It commemorates the willingness of Abraham to sacrifice his son Ishmael as an act of obedience to God. On this occasion, Muslims slaughter an animal (usually a sheep or a goat) and distribute its meat to their family, friends and the needy. They also visit cemeteries to pay respect to their deceased loved ones.

Cultural Festivals: Turkey has many cultural festivals that showcase its artistic, musical or culinary diversity and richness. Some of these festivals are:

Istanbul International Film Festival. This is the oldest and most prestigious film festival in Turkey, which takes place every April in Istanbul. It features screenings of local and international films, as well as competitions, workshops, panels and awards. It attracts filmmakers, critics and cinephiles from all over the world.

Aspendos International Opera and Ballet Festival. This is a unique festival that takes place every June and July in the ancient Roman theatre of Aspendos, near Antalya. It features performances of opera and ballet by renowned artists and companies from Turkey and abroad. It offers a spectacular experience of watching classical art in a historical setting.

Cappadox. This is a contemporary art and music festival that takes place every May or June in Cappadocia, the fairy-tale region of central Turkey. It features exhibitions, concerts, workshops and outdoor activities that blend with the natural and cultural landscape of Cappadocia. It attracts artists, musicians and visitors who seek inspiration and adventure.

Camel Wrestling Festival. This is a traditional festival that takes place every winter in various towns and villages along the Aegean coast of Turkey. It involves male camels wrestling with each other for the attention of a female camel in heat. It is a spectacle of strength, skill and endurance, as well as a celebration of local culture, food and music.

We hope this section helps you enjoy the festivals and celebrations in Turkey. Have a fun time!

Chapter 4 • Exploring Turkey's Regions

Istanbul

Istanbul is a city unlike any other. Straddling two continents, Europe and Asia, it is a place where ancient history and modern culture collide. Istanbul was once the capital of three empires: Roman, Byzantine and Ottoman, and its rich heritage can be seen in its stunning architecture, diverse cuisine and vibrant art scene. If you want to marvel at the majestic Hagia

Sophia, shop for souvenirs at the Grand Bazaar, cruise along the Bosphorus Strait or enjoy a night out at one of the many trendy bars and restaurants, Istanbul is the perfect place.

The best time to visit Istanbul is in spring or autumn when the weather is pleasant and the crowds are thinner. You can also catch the Tulip Festival in April when the city's parks are filled with colorful flowers. Summer can be hot and humid, but also lively and festive, while winter can be cold and rainy, but also atmospheric and cosy.

Istanbul is divided into several districts, each with its character and attractions. The most popular area for tourists is Sultanahmet, the historic heart of the city, where you can find the iconic Blue Mosque, the awe-inspiring Topkapi Palace, the mysterious Basilica Cistern and many other landmarks. Nearby is Eminönü, where you can catch a ferry to the Asian side of the city, or visit the Spice Bazaar for some aromatic treats. Across the Golden Horn is Beyoğlu, the modern and cosmopolitan district, where you can stroll along Istiklal Street, the main shopping and entertainment avenue, or explore the bohemian neighbourhoods of Galata, Karaköy and Cihangir. Further north is Beşiktaş, a lively area with many cafes, bars and restaurants, as well as the Dolmabahçe Palace, the former residence of the Ottoman sultans. On the Asian side, you can visit Kadıköy, a trendy and hip district with vibrant nightlife and a great food scene, or Üsküdar, a more traditional and conservative area with beautiful mosques and views of the Bosphorus.

Istanbul has a variety of transportation options to get around the city. You can use the metro, tram, bus or ferry to reach most destinations or take a taxi or Uber for more convenience. You can also rent a bike or walk to enjoy the scenery and atmosphere of the city. Just be aware that Istanbul is very large and traffic can be heavy at times, so plan your itinerary accordingly.

Istanbul is a city that will enchant you with its beauty, charm and energy. It is a place where you can experience different cultures, cuisines and lifestyles in one day. It is a place where you can discover something new every time you visit. It is a place that will make you fall in love with it over and over again.

Must-see Attractions in Istanbul

Istanbul is a city that offers countless attractions for visitors of all interests and tastes. From historical monuments to modern museums, from lively markets to scenic cruises, from religious sites to cultural events, there is something for everyone in this fascinating city. Below are some of the must-see attractions in Istanbul that you should not miss:

Hagia Sophia Mosque: This is one of the most iconic landmarks of Istanbul, which has served as a church, a mosque and a museum throughout its history. It was built in the 6th century by Emperor Justinian as a magnificent cathedral and was later converted into a mosque by the Ottomans in the 15th century. It is now a museum that showcases the stunning architecture, mosaics and frescoes of both Byzantine and Islamic art. It is also a UNESCO World Heritage Site, along with other historic areas of Istanbul.

Topkapi Palace: This is another UNESCO World Heritage Site, which was the imperial residence and administrative centre of the Ottoman sultans for almost 400 years. It is a complex of buildings, courtyards, gardens and pavilions that display the opulence, power and culture of the Ottoman Empire. You can see the lavish chambers, halls, treasury, harem, library and armoury of the palace, as well as the sacred relics of Islam, such as the Prophet Muhammad's cloak and sword.

Blue Mosque: This is one of the most beautiful mosques in Istanbul, which was built by Sultan Ahmet I in the 17th century to rival the Hagia Sophia. It is also known as the Sultanahmet Mosque, as it is located in the Sultanahmet district. It is famous for its six minarets and its blue-tiled interior, which features more than 20,000 handmade ceramic tiles. It is still an active place of worship, but visitors are welcome to enter outside prayer times.

Grand Bazaar: This is one of the oldest and largest covered markets in the world, which dates back to the 15th century. It is a labyrinth of more than 4,000 shops, stalls, workshops and cafes that sell everything from carpets, jewellery, spices, antiques, leather goods, souvenirs and more. It is a colourful and chaotic place where you can bargain with vendors, enjoy Turkish tea or coffee, or simply soak up the atmosphere.

Basilica Cistern: This is one of the most unusual attractions in Istanbul, which is an underground water reservoir that was built by Emperor Justinian in the 6th century. It is also known as the Sunken Palace or Yerebatan Sarayi in Turkish. It has a capacity of 80,000 cubic meters of water and is supported by 336 marble columns. It also features two Medusa heads at its base, which are believed to have been taken from ancient Roman buildings. You can walk along the wooden platforms that cross the cistern and admire its mysterious beauty.

Bosphorus Cruise: This is one of the best ways to enjoy the scenic views of Istanbul from both sides of the Bosphorus Strait, which separates Europe and Asia. You can take a public ferry or a private yacht and sail along the waterway that connects the Black Sea and the Sea of Marmara. You can see some of the landmarks of Istanbul along the way, such as the Dolmabahce Palace, the Ortakoy Mosque, the Rumeli Fortress and the Maiden's Tower. You can also stop at some of the charming villages and towns on both shores.

Chora Church: This is one of the most impressive Byzantine churches in Istanbul, which was originally built in the 4th century and later renovated in the 14th century by Theodore Metochites, a Byzantine statesman and patron of art. It is also known as Kariye Museum or Kariye Camii in Turkish. It is famous for its exquisite mosaics and frescoes that depict scenes from the life of Christ and the Virgin Mary. They are considered to be among the finest examples of Byzantine art in the world.

Galata Tower: This is one of the most recognizable landmarks of Istanbul, which was built by the Genoese in 1348 as part of their defensive wall. It is a medieval stone tower that stands 67 meters high and offers panoramic views of Istanbul from its observation deck. You can also enjoy a meal or a drink at its restaurant or cafe on top.

Istanbul Modern Museum: This is one of the most popular museums in Istanbul, which showcases the contemporary art and culture of Turkey and the world. It is located in a former warehouse on the shores of the Bosphorus and features permanent and temporary exhibitions of paintings, sculptures, photographs, videos and installations by Turkish and international artists. It also has a cinema, a library, a shop and a cafe.

Princes' Islands: These are a group of nine islands in the Sea of Marmara, which are a popular getaway from the hustle and bustle of Istanbul. They are known for their peaceful and picturesque atmosphere, as motor vehicles are banned on the islands. You can explore them by bike, horse-drawn carriage or on foot. You can also enjoy the beaches, parks, monasteries and mansions on the islands. The largest and most visited island is Büyükada, which means "Big Island" in Turkish.

We hope this section helps you plan your itinerary in Istanbul. Have a great time!

Recommendations for Accommodation

If you are planning to visit Istanbul, you might be wondering where to stay and what kind of accommodation suits your needs and budget. Below are some recommendations for different types of hotels in Istanbul, based on their location, amenities, and experiences.

Luxury Hotels

If you want to splurge on a lavish stay in Istanbul, you can choose from several five-star hotels that offer impeccable service, elegant rooms, and world-class facilities. Some of the best luxury hotels in Istanbul are:

Four Seasons Hotel Istanbul at Sultanahmet: This hotel is located in the heart of the historic district, within walking distance of the Hagia Sophia, the Blue Mosque, and the Topkapi Palace. It is housed in a former Ottoman prison that has been beautifully restored and decorated with Turkish art and antiques. The hotel features a rooftop terrace with panoramic views of the city, a courtyard garden with a fountain, a spa, a fitness centre, and a restaurant serving Mediterranean cuisine.

Çırağan Palace Kempinski Istanbul: This hotel is situated on the shores of the Bosphorus, in a former Ottoman palace that dates back to the 19th century. It offers a royal experience with its opulent rooms and suites, some of which have balconies or terraces overlooking the water. The hotel also boasts an infinity pool, a private pier, a helipad, a spa, a fitness centre, and several restaurants and bars, including one that serves authentic Ottoman dishes.

Swissotel The Bosphorus Istanbul: This hotel is located in the lively Taksim area, close to many shops, restaurants, and attractions. It has a modern design with spacious rooms and suites that have floor-to-ceiling windows and balconies with stunning views of the city and the Bosphorus. The hotel also has an exclusive rooftop pool, an award-winning spa, a fitness centre, a tennis court, a golf simulator, and several dining options.

Boutique Hotels

If you prefer a more intimate and personalized stay in Istanbul, you can opt for one of the many boutique hotels that offer charm, character, and style. Some of the best boutique hotels in Istanbul are:

Witt Istanbul Suites: This hotel is located in the trendy Cihangir neighbourhood, known for its cafes, galleries, and antique shops. It has 18 stylish suites that feature contemporary design with retro touches, kitchenettes, marble bathrooms, and balconies with city or sea views. The hotel also has a cosy lobby lounge with a fireplace, a library, and a terrace garden.

Ibrahim Pasha Hotel: This hotel is located in the historic Sultanahmet district, just steps away from the Blue Mosque and the Hagia Sophia. It is housed in two Ottoman townhouses that have been renovated with modern amenities and tasteful decor. The hotel has 24 cosy rooms that have wooden floors, Turkish rugs, and comfortable beds. The hotel also has a rooftop terrace with spectacular views of the old city and the Bosphorus.

Sumahan On The Water: This hotel is located on the Asian side of Istanbul, on the edge of the Bosphorus. It is a former distillery that has been transformed into a chic boutique hotel with 24 spacious rooms and suites that have minimalist designs.

Recommendations for Restaurants

Istanbul is a culinary paradise that offers a variety of dishes influenced by its diverse cultures, history, and geography. You can find everything from street food to fine dining, from traditional Turkish cuisine to international flavours, from seafood to vegetarian options. Below are some recommendations for different types of restaurants in Istanbul, based on their location, quality, and experiences.

Fine Dining Restaurants

If you want to treat yourself to a memorable dining experience in Istanbul, you can choose from several fine dining restaurants that have been awarded Michelin stars or Bib Gourmands. Some of the best fine-dining restaurants in Istanbul are:

Turk Fatih Tutak: This is the only restaurant in Istanbul that has received two Michelin stars and for good reason. Chef Fatih Tutak creates a daily tasting menu that showcases the best of Turkish ingredients, techniques, and flavours, with a modern and international twist. The dishes are beautifully presented and paired with exquisite wines. The restaurant also has stylish decor and a stunning view of the Bosphorus.

Mikla: This restaurant is located on the rooftop of the Marmara Pera Hotel, and offers breathtaking views of the city, including the Hagia Sophia and the Topkapi Palace. Chef Mehmet Gürs serves contemporary Anatolian cuisine that blends Turkish traditions with Scandinavian influences. The menu changes seasonally and features local and organic products. The restaurant also has a chic bar and a terrace.

Nicole: This restaurant is situated in a historic building that was once a Franciscan monastery, and has a cosy atmosphere and a lovely garden. Chef Aylin Yazıcıoğlu prepares a Mediterranean-inspired cuisine that uses fresh and seasonal ingredients from the nearby islands and farms. The menu changes every six weeks and offers a choice of four or six courses, with optional wine pairings. The restaurant also has an impressive wine cellar with over 600 labels.

Casual Dining Restaurants

If you prefer a more relaxed and affordable dining experience in Istanbul, you can opt for one of the many casual dining restaurants that offer delicious food, friendly service, and a cosy ambience. Some of the best casual dining restaurants in Istanbul are:

Lekker Ottoman Cuisine: This restaurant is located in the historic Sultanahmet district, near the main attractions. It specializes in Ottoman cuisine, which is influenced by various regions and cultures of the former empire. The menu features dishes such as lamb stew with dried apricots, chicken with walnut sauce, stuffed vine leaves, and baklava. The restaurant also has a terrace with a view of the Hagia Sophia.

Mivan Restaurant Cafe: This restaurant is located in the lively Beyoglu area, near the Galata Tower. It serves a fusion of Mediterranean and Turkish cuisine, with dishes such as falafel burgers, chicken casserole, hummus, and spicy sauce. The restaurant also has a cafe section that offers coffee, tea, desserts, and shisha.

Resto Ethnica: This restaurant is located in the trendy Karakoy neighborhood, near the Bosphorus. It offers a variety of ethnic dishes from different countries, such as Moroccan couscous, Indian curry, Thai noodles, and Mexican tacos. The restaurant also has a wine bar that serves local and international wines.

Ankara

Ankara is the capital of Turkey and the second-largest city in the country after Istanbul. It is a modern and cosmopolitan city that reflects Turkey's economic and political importance on the world stage. Ankara is also a city of culture, history and nature, offering a variety of attractions and activities for visitors.

One of the main reasons to visit Ankara is to learn more about Turkey's fascinating past, from the ancient civilizations that inhabited Anatolia to the modern republic founded by Mustafa Kemal Atatürk. The Museum of Anatolian Civilizations is a must-see for anyone interested in archaeology and history, as it displays a superb collection of artefacts from different periods and regions of Turkey. The Anıt Kabir is another impressive monument that honours Atatürk, the father of the Turkish nation and houses his mausoleum, museum and ceremonial grounds.

Ankara also has some beautiful examples of Ottoman and Islamic architecture, such as the Hacı Bayram Mosque, the Kocatepe Mosque and the Citadel, which dates back to the Byzantine era and offers panoramic views of the city. The Ethnography Museum and the Vakıf Eserleri Museum showcase the rich cultural heritage of Turkey, with exhibits of traditional crafts, costumes, carpets and musical instruments.

For those who want to enjoy some green spaces and nature in Ankara, there are several options to choose from. The Gençlik Parkı is a large and popular park in the centre of the city, with a lake, fountains, playgrounds and cafes. The Atatürk Forest Farm and Zoo is a recreational area that combines agriculture, wildlife and leisure facilities. The Eymir Lake is a scenic spot for picnics, fishing and boating, while the

Kızılcahamam-Çamlıdere National Park is a natural reserve with thermal springs, forests and hiking trails.

Ankara also has a lively and diverse culinary scene, with restaurants serving dishes from different regions of Turkey as well as international cuisines. Some of the local specialities to try are döner kebab, Ankara tava (lamb stew), çiğ köfte (raw meatballs), gözleme (stuffed flatbread) and ayran (yoghurt drink). For dessert, don't miss the famous Ankara baklava or the Angora ice cream made from goat's milk. To experience the nightlife of Ankara, head to Kızılay or Kavaklıdere districts, where you can find bars, pubs, clubs and live music venues.

Ankara is a city that offers something for everyone, whether you are looking for culture, history, nature or entertainment. It is a city that will surprise you with its dynamism, diversity and charm.

Must-see Attractions in Ankara

Ankara is not only the capital of Turkey, but also a city with many cultural, historical, and natural attractions. Whether you are interested in ancient civilizations, modern art, or scenic parks, you will find something to suit your taste in Ankara. Below are some of the must-see attractions in Ankara that you should not miss.

Ankara Castle is a medieval fortress that dominates the skyline of the old city. It dates back to the Hittite period but was expanded and renovated by various civilizations over time, such as the Romans, Byzantines, Seljuqs, Mongols, and Ottomans. You can walk along the walls and towers of the castle and enjoy the panoramic views of the city and the surrounding mountains. Inside the castle, you can also explore the citadel district, where you can see traditional Ottoman houses, mosques, museums, and handicraft shops.

Anıtkabir is the mausoleum of Mustafa Kemal Atatürk, the founder of the Republic of Turkey and its first president. It is a symbol of Turkish nationalism and a popular destination for visitors and pilgrims. The mausoleum is located on a hilltop, surrounded by a vast plaza and a park. It has a monumental architecture that combines Turkish and Western styles, with marble columns, reliefs, mosaics, and statues. Inside the mausoleum, you can see the sarcophagus of Atatürk and his personal belongings. Next to the mausoleum, there is a museum complex that displays exhibits about Atatürk's life and legacy, as well as the history of Turkey.

The Museum of Anatolian Civilizations is one of the best museums in Turkey and in the world. It showcases the artefacts from various ancient civilizations that inhabited Anatolia, such as the Hittites, Phrygians, Lydians, Persians, Greeks, Romans, Byzantines, Seljuqs, Mongols, Ottomans, and Turks. The museum is located in two Ottoman buildings near Ankara Castle. It has a rich collection of pottery, jewellery, sculptures, reliefs, inscriptions, coins, seals, weapons, and more. Some of the highlights include the wall painting from Çatalhöyük (thought to be the world's first town map), the fertility goddess statue from Çatalhöyük (one of the oldest human representations), the clay tablets from Hattuşa (the capital of the Hittite Empire), and the gold ornaments from Alacahöyük (a Phrygian royal tomb).

Recommendations for Accommodation

Ankara offers a wide range of accommodation options for different budgets and preferences. You can find luxury hotels, boutique hotels, budget hotels, and hostels in various locations of the city. Below are some recommendations for different types of accommodation in Ankara, based on their quality, service, and experiences.

Luxury Hotels

If you want to enjoy a comfortable and elegant stay in Ankara, you can choose from several five-star hotels that provide excellent facilities, amenities, and service. Some of the best luxury hotels in Ankara are:

JW Marriott Hotel Ankara: This hotel is located in the Söğütözü business district, close to the Armada shopping centre and the Congresium convention centre. It has 413 spacious rooms and suites that feature modern design, marble bathrooms, and city views. The hotel also has an indoor pool, a spa, a fitness centre, and several restaurants and bars.

Wyndham Ankara: This hotel is situated in the Söğütözü business district, opposite the Armada shopping centre and near the Congresium convention centre. It has 138 stylish rooms and suites that have ergonomic work desks, minibars, and free Wi-Fi. The hotel also has an indoor pool, a sauna, a fitness centre, and a restaurant serving Turkish and international cuisine.

Lugal, A Luxury Collection Hotel: This hotel is located in the Kavaklıdere district, near Tunali Hilmi Avenue and Kugulu Park. It has 91 elegant rooms and suites that have luxurious bedding, Nespresso machines, and Bosphorus or city views. The hotel also has an outdoor pool, a spa, a fitness centre, and two restaurants serving French and Turkish cuisine.

Boutique Hotels

If you prefer a more intimate and personalized stay in Ankara, you can opt for one of the many boutique hotels that offer charm, character, and style. Some of the best boutique hotels in Ankara are:

Divan Cukurhan: This hotel is located in the citadel district, near the Museum of Anatolian Civilizations and the Ankara Castle. It is housed in a historic caravanserai that has been restored with modern amenities and tasteful decor. The hotel has 19 cosy rooms that have wooden floors, antique furniture, and fireplaces. The hotel also has a terrace with castle views, a library, and a restaurant serving Anatolian cuisine.

Point Hotel Ankara: This hotel is located in the Çankaya district, near Kızılay Square and Kugulu Park.

It has 162 chic rooms and suites that feature contemporary design, smart TVs, and free Wi-Fi. The hotel also has an indoor pool, a spa, a fitness centre, and a restaurant serving Mediterranean cuisine.

Aldino Residence: This hotel is located in the Maltepe district, near the Kızılay Square and the Anıtkabir. It has 32 spacious rooms that have kitchenettes, living areas, balconies, and free Wi-Fi. The hotel also has a garden with a fountain, a terrace with city views, and a cafe serving breakfast and snacks.

Recommendations for Restaurants

Ankara is a culinary paradise that offers a variety of dishes influenced by its diverse cultures, history, and geography. You can find everything from street food to fine dining, from traditional Turkish cuisine to international flavours, from kebabs to seafood. Below are some recommendations for different types of restaurants in Ankara, based on their quality, service, and experiences.

Fine Dining Restaurants

If you want to treat yourself to a memorable dining experience in Ankara, you can choose from several fine dining restaurants that have been awarded Michelin stars or Bib Gourmands. Some of the best fine-dining restaurants in Ankara are:

L'avare: This restaurant is located in the Çankaya district, near Kugulu Park. It is run by a Michelin-starred Italian chef who creates a daily tasting menu that showcases the best of Turkish ingredients, techniques, and flavours, with a modern and international twist. The dishes are beautifully presented and paired with exquisite wines. The restaurant also has a cosy bar and a terrace.

Trilye Restaurant: This restaurant is situated in the Söğütözü district, near the Congresium convention centre. It specializes in seafood and Mediterranean cuisine, with dishes such as grilled octopus, sea bass carpaccio, shrimp casserole, and fish soup. The restaurant also has an extensive wine list and a garden.

No4 Restaurant Bar Lounge: This restaurant is located in the Kavaklıdere district, near Tunali Hilmi Avenue and the Lugal Hotel. It serves contemporary European cuisine that blends Turkish traditions with French influences. The menu features dishes such as duck confit, lamb shank, beef Wellington, and chocolate soufflé. The restaurant also has a chic bar and a lounge.

Casual Dining Restaurants

If you prefer a more relaxed and affordable dining experience in Ankara, you can opt for one of the many casual dining restaurants that offer delicious food, friendly service, and a cosy ambience. Some of the best casual dining restaurants in Ankara are:

Pizzeria Alla Torre: This restaurant is located in the Ulus district, near the Temple of Augustus and Rome. It serves authentic Italian pizza with a thin crust and fresh toppings. You can choose from various pizza options or create your own. The restaurant also offers salads, pasta, desserts, and drinks.

Duveroglu: This restaurant is located in the Kızılay district, near the Kızılay Square and the Anıtkabir. It is one of the most popular places to try Turkish fast food, such as döner (meat cooked on a vertical spit), pide (flatbread with various fillings), lahmacun (thin-crust pizza with minced meat and spices), and ayran (yoghurt drink). The restaurant also serves soups, salads, desserts, and tea.

Masabasi Kebapcisi: This restaurant is located in the Kızılay district, near Mithatpaşa Avenue and the Pecenek Döner. It offers a variety of kebabs (grilled meat on skewers or plates), such as Adana kebab (spicy minced lamb), Urfa kebab (mild minced lamb), şiş kebab (cubed lamb or chicken), and best kebab (minced meat wrapped in lavash bread). The restaurant also serves meze (appetizers), salads, rice, bread, and drinks.

Izmir

Izmir is a city on the Aegean coast of Turkey that has a long and rich history, a lively and cosmopolitan culture, and a stunning natural setting. Izmir is the third-largest city in Turkey and one of the oldest in the world, dating back to ancient times when it was known as Smyrna. Izmir is also a gateway to some of the most famous attractions in Turkey, such as Ephesus, Pergamon and Pamukkale.

One of the main attractions of Izmir is its seafront promenade, called the Kordon, which stretches for several kilometres along the bay and offers beautiful views of the water and the mountains. The Kordon is a popular place for locals and visitors to walk, bike, jog or relax in one of the many cafes, restaurants and bars that line the shore. The Kordon also connects some of the most interesting areas of the city, such as Konak, where you can find the iconic clock tower and the bustling bazaar, Alsancak, where you can enjoy the modern and trendy nightlife, and Karşıyaka, where you can take a ferry to the other side of the bay.

Izmir also has a wealth of historical and cultural sights to explore, such as the Izmir Museum of History and Art, which displays a superb collection of artefacts from different periods and regions of Turkey, the Agora, which is the ancient marketplace of Smyrna that was rebuilt by Alexander the Great, the Church of St Polycarp, which is the oldest Christian church in the city and a symbol of its multicultural heritage, and the Kadifekale, which is a hilltop castle that offers panoramic views of the city.

Izmir also has plenty of natural attractions to enjoy, such as the Bird Paradise in Çiğli, which is a wetland area that hosts hundreds of species of birds, the İnciraltı City Forest, which is a green oasis with walking trails and picnic areas, and the Balçova Thermal Baths, which are natural hot springs that offer healing and relaxation. For a day trip, you can visit some of the nearby wonders of Turkey, such as Ephesus, which is one of the best-preserved ancient cities in the world and a UNESCO World Heritage Site, Pergamon, which is another ancient city that boasts impressive temples and acropolis, and Pamukkale, which is a natural phenomenon of white travertine terraces filled with mineral-rich water.

Izmir is a city that will impress you with its history, culture and nature. It is a city that will make you feel welcome and comfortable. It is a city that will make you want to come back again.

Must-see Attractions in Izmir

Izmir is a charming city on the Aegean coast of Turkey, with a rich history, culture, and cuisine. If you are looking for some must-see attractions in Izmir, you will not be disappointed. Below are some of the best places to visit in Izmir, Turkey, for a memorable experience.

Konak Square and Clock Tower

This is the iconic landmark of Izmir, located in the Konak district by the sea. The square is a lively and colourful place, where you can see the locals and tourists mingling, enjoying the views, and taking photos. The clock tower is a beautiful structure that was built in 1901 to commemorate the 25th anniversary of Sultan Abdulhamid II's reign. It has four fountains around it and a Moorish-style design. The clock tower is also illuminated at night, creating a romantic atmosphere.

Kemeralti Bazaar

This is the oldest and largest bazaar in Izmir, dating back to the 17th century. It is a maze of narrow streets, lined with shops, stalls, cafes, mosques, synagogues, and hammams. You can find anything here, from spices and souvenirs to clothes and jewellery. The bazaar is also a great place to experience the local culture, as you can hear the call to prayer, smell Turkish coffee, and taste the street food.

Agora

This is the ancient marketplace of Izmir, located in the Namazgah neighbourhood. It was built by Alexander the Great in the 4th century BC and later rebuilt by Marcus Aurelius in the 2nd century AD after an earthquake. The agora was a centre of commerce, politics, and social life in Roman times. You can still see the impressive arches, columns, and fountains that remain from the original structure. You can also explore the underground chambers and tunnels that were used for storage and water supply.

Ephesus

This is one of the most famous and visited ancient sites in Turkey, located about 80 km from Izmir. Ephesus was once a thriving city on the Silk Road, with a population of over 250,000 people. It was also home to the Temple of Artemis, one of the Seven Wonders of the Ancient World. Today, you can marvel at the well-preserved ruins of Ephesus, such as the Library of Celsus, the Grand Theater, the Odeon, and the Terrace Houses. You can also visit the nearby House of the Virgin Mary, where Mary is believed to have spent her last years.

Pergamon Acropolis

This is another impressive ancient site in Turkey, located about 100 km from Izmir. Pergamon was once a powerful kingdom that rivalled Rome and Alexandria in culture and science. It was also famous for its library, which contained over 200,000 scrolls. The Acropolis of Pergamon is situated on a hilltop overlooking the modern town of Bergama. You can see the remains of temples, palaces, theatres, altars, and fortifications that testify to the glory of Pergamon.

Hierapolis-Pamukkale

This is a UNESCO World Heritage Site that combines natural beauty and historical significance. Pamukkale means "cotton castle" in Turkish and refers to the white travertine terraces that are formed by mineral-rich hot springs. The terraces have pools of turquoise water that are open for bathing and offer stunning views of the valley below. Hierapolis is an ancient city that was built on top of Pamukkale by the Romans in the 2nd century BC. It was a spa town that attracted people for its healing waters and religious sites. You can see the ruins of temples, baths, tombs, theatres, and churches in Hierapolis.

Village of Sirince

This is a quaint village in the hills near Selcuk, about 90 km from Izmir. It is known for its traditional stone houses, cobblestone streets, and fruit wines. Sirince was originally inhabited by Greeks until 1924 when they were exchanged with Turks from Thessaloniki as part of a population exchange agreement between Turkey and Greece. The village has preserved its Greek heritage and charm and attracts visitors who want to experience a rural lifestyle.

Kordonboyu

This is the waterfront promenade of Izmir that stretches for about 6 km along the Aegean Sea. It is a popular place for locals and tourists to walk, bike, jog, or relax on the grassy areas or benches. You can also enjoy the sea breeze, watch the sunset or sunrise over the water, and admire the yachts and ships that dock at the port. Along the Kordonboyu, you can find many cafes, restaurants, bars, and clubs that offer a variety of food and entertainment options.

Tarihi Asansor

This is a historical elevator that was built in 1907 by a Jewish businessman named Nesim Levi Bayraklioglu. It connects the two neighbourhoods of Karatas and Halil Rifat Pasa, which are separated by a cliff. The elevator was originally powered by water and later by electricity. It has a height of 51 meters and offers panoramic views of Izmir from the top. There is also a cafe and a restaurant at the top, where you can enjoy a drink or a meal with a view.

Izmir Wildlife Park

This is a modern zoo that covers an area of 425,000 square meters in the Sasali district of Izmir. It is home to over 1,500 animals from 120 different species, such as lions, tigers, bears, giraffes, zebras, monkeys, and birds. The zoo is designed to mimic the natural habitats of the animals and to educate visitors about wildlife conservation. You can also enjoy the botanical garden, the aquarium, the reptile house, and the children's park in the zoo.

Recommendations for Accommodation

Izmir is a beautiful city on the Aegean coast of Turkey, with a rich history, culture, and cuisine. If you are planning to visit Izmir, you will need a comfortable and convenient place to stay. Below are some of the best hotels in Izmir, Turkey, for a luxurious stay.

Renaissance Izmir Hotel

This is a 5-star hotel in the heart of Izmir, close to the Kordon promenade and the historic Kemeralti bazaar. The hotel offers spacious and elegant rooms with sea or city views, LCD TVs, minibars, and free Wi-Fi. You can also enjoy the rooftop pool, the spa and wellness centre, the fitness centre, and the sauna. The hotel has two restaurants that serve Turkish and international cuisine, as well as a lobby bar and a rooftop bar.

Park Inn by Radisson Izmir

This is a 4-star hotel located a few steps from the Kordon coastline, with stunning views of the Aegean Sea. The hotel features modern and stylish rooms with LCD TVs, minibars, safes, and free Wi-Fi. You can also access the fitness centre, the business centre, and the terrace. The hotel has a restaurant that serves buffet breakfast and à la carte lunch and dinner, as well as a lobby bar and a terrace bar.

Swissotel Buyuk Efes Izmir

This is a 5-star hotel located in the centre of Izmir, overlooking the Aegean Sea. The hotel boasts luxurious and spacious rooms with LCD TVs, coffee makers, safes, and free Wi-Fi. You can also indulge in the indoor and outdoor pools, the spa and wellness centre, the fitness centre, and the tennis court. The hotel has five restaurants that offer a variety of cuisines, from Turkish to Japanese to Mediterranean, as well as four bars and lounges.

Wyndham Grand İzmir Özdilek

This is a 5-star hotel located on the shore of İzmir Bay, with panoramic views of the sea and the city. The hotel provides elegant and comfortable rooms with LCD TVs, minibars, safes, and free Wi-Fi. You can also enjoy the outdoor pool, the spa and wellness centre, the fitness centre, and the sauna. The hotel has two restaurants that serve Turkish and international dishes, as well as two bars and a patisserie.

Orty Airport Hotel

This is a 4-star hotel located at the entrance of the İzmir Adnan Menderes International Airport, making it ideal for travellers who need to catch an early flight or arrive late at night. The hotel offers cosy and clean rooms with LCD TVs, minibars, safes, and free Wi-Fi. You can also use the fitness centre and the business centre. The hotel has a restaurant that serves buffet breakfast and à la carte lunch and dinner, as well as a lobby bar.

DoubleTree By Hilton Izmir Airport

This is a 4-star hotel located near the İzmir Adnan Menderes International Airport, offering convenience and comfort for travellers. The hotel features contemporary and spacious rooms with LCD TVs, coffee makers, safes, and free Wi-Fi. You can also access the outdoor pool, the fitness centre, and the business centre. The hotel has a restaurant that serves buffet breakfast and à la carte lunch and dinner, as well as a lobby bar.

Recommendations for Restaurants

Izmir is a city that offers a variety of cuisines, from traditional Turkish dishes to international flavours. If you are looking for some recommendations for restaurants in Izmir, you will have plenty of options to choose from. Below are some of the best restaurants in Izmir, Turkey, for a satisfying meal.

Tavaci Recep Usta

This is one of the best kebab restaurants in Izmir, located in the Alsancak district by the sea. The restaurant serves delicious meat and kebab dishes, such as tandoori, ribs, and doners. You can also enjoy dessert and tea after your meal, such as baklava and semolina halva. The restaurant has a nice view of the sea and the greenery of the Kordon promenade. It is open every day from 8:30 AM to 10 PM.

La Cigale

This is a French restaurant located next to the French Cultural Center in the Alsancak district. The restaurant offers a taste of French culture and cuisine, with dishes such as escargot, foie gras, steak frites, and crème brûlée. You can also sip wine or cocktails in a stylish garden ambience. The restaurant is closed on Sundays and open every other day from 11 AM to 12 AM.

Cafe Plaza Brasserie Bomonti

This is a lively place located on Gul Street, the busiest place in Alsancak. The cafe is a great place for celebrations, as it often features live music and DJs. You can also enjoy beer varieties, wine, and other drinks, as well as snacks and appetizers. The cafe has a vibrant atmosphere and a friendly staff. It is open every day from 10 AM to 2 AM.

Less Ordinary

This is a cosy and charming place located in the Karsiyaka district. The restaurant serves Mediterranean and Turkish cuisine, with dishes such as salads, soups, pasta, pizza, burgers, and meatballs. You can also try their homemade desserts, such as cheesecake, brownies, and tiramisu. The restaurant has an amazing atmosphere with vintage decor, books, plants, and candles. It is open every day from 9 AM to 11 PM.

%100 Cafe & More

This is a modern and spacious place located in the Bostanli district. The cafe serves breakfast, brunch, lunch, and dinner, with dishes such as omelettes, pancakes, sandwiches, wraps, salads, pasta, steak, and fish. You can also enjoy coffee, tea, smoothies, cocktails, and wine. The cafe has a minimalist design with wooden furniture and colourful cushions. It is open every day from 8 AM to 12 AM.

North Pier's

This is a seafood restaurant located on the pier of Karsiyaka. The restaurant offers fresh and tasty seafood dishes, such as calamari, shrimp, octopus, mussels, sea bass, and salmon. You can also savour the sea view and the breeze while dining on the pier. The restaurant is open every day from 11 AM to 11 PM.

B'ready

This is a burger restaurant located in the Bornova district. The restaurant serves delicious hamburgers made with fresh ingredients and homemade sauces. You can choose from different types of burgers, such as classic cheeseburgers, mushroom burgers, chicken burgers, or veggie burgers. You can also order fries or onion rings as sides. The restaurant has a casual and fun vibe with colourful walls and posters. It is open every day from 11 AM to 11 PM.

Bursa

Bursa is a city in northwestern Turkey that was once the capital of the Ottoman Empire. It is a city of history, culture and nature, with many attractions to explore and enjoy. Bursa is famous for its silk production, thermal springs, delicious cuisine and green scenery.

One of the main highlights of Bursa is its historical centre, where you can admire the splendid mosques, mausoleums and bazaars that date back to the Ottoman era. The Ulu Cami (Grand Mosque) is the largest and most impressive mosque in the city, with 20 domes and a beautiful fountain. The Yeşil Cami (Green Mosque) and the Yeşil Türbe (Green Tomb) are also worth visiting for their exquisite tile work and architecture.

The Koza Han is a 15th-century caravanserai that now serves as a silk market, where you can buy colourful fabrics, scarves and carpets.

Bursa is also known for its natural beauty and outdoor activities. You can take a cable car to the summit of Mt Uludağ, Turkey's premier ski resort, where you can enjoy skiing, snowboarding or hiking in different seasons. You can also relax in one of the many thermal spas in the Çekirge district, where you can soak in mineral-rich waters and enjoy traditional Turkish baths. For a day trip, you can visit the nearby village of Cumalıkızık, a charming example of Ottoman rural life, with stone houses, cobblestone streets and a museum.

Bursa also has a vibrant and diverse culinary scene, with restaurants serving dishes from different regions of Turkey as well as international cuisines. Some of the local specialities to try are İskender kebab, a dish of sliced meat over bread with tomato sauce and yoghurt, Bursa kebabı, a type of grilled meat wrapped in thin bread, cantık, a stuffed pastry similar to pizza, and kemalpaşa tatlısı, a dessert made of cheese and syrup. Bursa is also famous for its chestnuts, peaches and cherries, which you can find in markets and street stalls.

Bursa is a city that will delight you with its historical charm, natural wonders and gastronomic delights. It is a city that will make you appreciate the legacy of the Ottoman Empire and the beauty of Turkey.

Must-see Attractions in Bursa

Bursa is a city that offers a variety of attractions for travellers who want to discover its history, culture, nature, and cuisine. Some of the must-see attractions in Bursa are:

The mausoleums of the early Ottoman sultans

These are the tombs of the founders and rulers of the Ottoman Empire, who made Bursa their first capital. They are located in different districts of Bursa and reflect the architectural styles of their respective periods. You can visit the mausoleums of Osman Gazi, Orhan Gazi, Murad I, Bayezid I, Mehmed I, and Murad II and learn about their lives and achievements.

The Green Mosque and the Green Tomb

These are two of the most beautiful monuments in Bursa, named after their green tiles and decorations. The mosque was built by Mehmed I in 1419 and is considered one of the finest examples of Ottoman architecture. It has a spacious interior with exquisite calligraphy, tiles, fountains, and a wooden pulpit. The tomb is located next to the mosque and contains the sarcophagus of Mehmed I. It has a hexagonal shape and a dome covered with green tiles.

The Koza Han

This is a historical caravanserai that was built by Bayezid II in 1491. It was used as a silk market and a resting place for travellers. Today, it is a popular place to shop for souvenirs, such as silk scarves, carpets, jewellery, and antiques. It also has a tranquil courtyard with a fountain and a mosque, where you can relax and enjoy a cup of tea.

The Mount Uludağ

This is a national park and a ski resort that overlooks Bursa. It is known as the Mysian Olympus or Bithynian Olympus in classical antiquity and has an elevation of 2,543 meters. It offers various activities for winter sports enthusiasts, such as skiing, snowboarding, sledging, and ice skating. You can also take the Bursa Teleferik cable car to reach the top station and enjoy the panoramic views of the city and the sea.

The Çekirge district

This is a famous district in Bursa for its thermal springs and baths that have been used since Roman times. Many hotels and spas offer treatments with mineral-rich water that is said to have healing properties for various ailments. You can also visit the historical baths, such as the Karamustafa Pasa Baths, the Eski Kaplica (Old Spring), and the Yeni Kaplica (New Spring).

The Cumalıkızık village

This is a UNESCO World Heritage Site that showcases the traditional Ottoman rural life. It is located about 10 km from Bursa and has well-preserved stone houses with colourful windows and doors. It also has a museum that displays local artefacts and customs. You can stroll around the village and taste its famous breakfast with local products.

The Ulu Cami (Grand Mosque)

This is the largest mosque in Bursa and one of the oldest in Turkey. It was built by Bayezid I in 1399 and has 20 domes and two minarets. It is famous for its calligraphy, tiles, fountains, and wooden pulpit. It also has a sacred relic, which is said to be a piece of Prophet Muhammad's beard

Recommendations for Accommodation

Bursa is a city that offers a variety of accommodation options for travellers who want to enjoy its history, culture, nature, and cuisine. You can find hotels, B&Bs, inns, and speciality lodgings that suit your budget and preferences. Below are some of the best hotels in Bursa, Turkey, for a comfortable stay.

Mövenpick Hotel & Thermal Spa Bursa

This is a 5-star hotel located in the centre of Bursa, close to the Ataturk Museum and the Kent Meydani Shopping Center. The hotel features luxurious and spacious rooms with LCD TVs, coffee makers, safes, and free Wi-Fi. You can also enjoy the indoor and outdoor pools, the spa and wellness centre, the fitness centre, and the sauna. The hotel has five restaurants that offer a variety of cuisines, from Turkish to Japanese to Mediterranean, as well as four bars and lounges.

Holiday Inn Bursa - City Centre, an IHG Hotel

This is a 4-star hotel located in the heart of Bursa, just a few steps from the Kent Meydani Shopping Center. The hotel offers cosy and elegant rooms with LCD TVs, minibars, safes, and free Wi-Fi. You can also access the fitness centre and the business centre. The hotel has a restaurant that serves buffet breakfast and à la carte lunch and dinner, as well as a lobby bar and a rooftop bar.

Almira Hotel Thermal Spa & Convention Center

This is a 5-star hotel located near the Ulu Cami (Grand Mosque) and the Koza Han (Cocoon Inn) in Bursa. The hotel boasts stylish and comfortable rooms with LCD TVs, minibars, safes, and free Wi-Fi. You can also enjoy the indoor pool, the spa and wellness centre, the fitness centre, and the hammam. The hotel has four restaurants that serve Turkish and international dishes, as well as three bars and a patisserie.

Kitapevi Hotel

This is a boutique hotel located in a historical building in the old town of Bursa. The hotel offers charming and cosy rooms with LCD TVs, minibars, safes, and free Wi-Fi. You can also relax in the garden or the library. The hotel has a restaurant that serves buffet breakfast and à la carte lunch and dinner, as well as a cafe that offers snacks and drinks.

Eleia Hotel İznik

This is a small hotel located in the village of Iznik, about 80 km from Bursa. Iznik is famous for its pottery and its historical sites, such as the Hagia Sophia Church and the Iznik Lake. The hotel offers lovely and clean rooms with LCD TVs, minibars, safes, and free Wi-Fi. You can also enjoy the outdoor pool, the garden, and the terrace. The hotel has a restaurant that serves buffet breakfast and à la carte lunch and dinner, as well as a bar that offers drinks and cocktails.

Recommendations for Restaurants

Bursa is a city that offers a variety of cuisines, from traditional Turkish dishes to international flavours. You can find restaurants that suit your taste buds and budget in different districts of Bursa. Below are some of the best restaurants in Bursa for a satisfying meal.

Selçuk Restaurant

This is one of the oldest and most popular restaurants in Bursa, located in the Alsancak district by the sea. The restaurant serves delicious Turkish and international dishes, such as kebabs, salads, soups, pasta, steak, and fish. You can also enjoy dessert and tea after your meal, such as baklava, chocolate soufflé, and panna cotta. The restaurant has a nice view of the sea and the greenery of the Kordon promenade. It is open every day from 8:30 AM to 10 PM.

Beyaz Kayaler

This is a seafood restaurant located in the coastal town of Mudanya, about 20 miles outside of Bursa. The restaurant offers beautiful sea views and a menu brimming with fresh Meditterranean and Aegean inspired dishes. You can also expect specialities like shrimp manti, sea bass wrapped in chard or scallops with white wine sauce.

Haskoyum Pidecisi

This is a cosy and charming place that has been serving its signature dish since 1998. Pide, which is a Turkish recipe, is its signature dish. It is similar to pizza featuring flatbread with a range of tasty toppings. You can also try their homemade desserts, such as cheesecake, brownies, and tiramisu. The restaurant has an amazing atmosphere with vintage decor, books, plants, and candles. It is open every day from 9 AM to 11 PM.

Uzan Et Mangal

This is a family-friendly steak-house, grill and barbecue restaurant that serves tender steaks, juicy chops, and succulent kebabs. You can also enjoy coffee, tea, smoothies, cocktails, and wine. The cafe has a minimalist design with wooden furniture and colourful cushions. It is open every day from 8 AM to 12 AM.

Antalya

Antalya is a city on the Mediterranean coast of Turkey that is known as the gateway to the Turkish Riviera and the Turquoise Coast. It is a city that combines ancient history, modern culture and stunning nature, with many attractions and activities to suit every taste. Antalya is the fifth-largest city in Turkey and one of the most popular tourist destinations in the country.

One of the main attractions of Antalya is its old town, called Kaleiçi, which is a maze of narrow streets, colourful houses and historical monuments. Here you can admire the Yivli Minaret Mosque, the symbol of the city, the Hadrian's Gate, a triumphal arch built by the Roman emperor, the Clock Tower, a landmark from the Ottoman era, and the Hıdırlık Tower, a stone tower overlooking the sea. You can also visit the Antalya Museum, which displays a superb collection of artefacts from different periods and regions of Turkey, especially from the nearby archaeological sites.

Antalya also has a beautiful coastline, with sandy beaches, rocky coves and clear blue water. You can enjoy swimming, sunbathing, surfing, diving or sailing on one of the many beaches in and around the city, such as Konyaaltı, Lara, Kaputaş or Olympos. You can also take a boat trip to explore the islands, bays and caves along the coast, or join a cruise to visit some of the most famous attractions in Turkey, such as Ephesus, Pamukkale or Cappadocia.

Antalya also has plenty of natural attractions to enjoy, such as the Düden Waterfalls, which are two spectacular cascades that drop into the sea from a cliff, the Köprülü Canyon, which is a scenic gorge where you can go rafting or hiking, and the Saklıkent Ski Center, which is a winter resort on the slopes of Mount Taurus. For a day trip, you can visit some of the nearby historical sites, such as Aspendos, which is an ancient city with one of the best-preserved Roman theatres in the world, Perge, which is another ancient city with impressive ruins and mosaics, and Termessos, which is an ancient mountain city with stunning views.

Antalya is a city that will impress you with its history, culture and nature. It is a city that will make you feel relaxed and entertained. It is a city that will make you want to discover more of Turkey.

Must-see Attractions in Antalya

Antalya is a city that has a lot to offer for travellers who want to see its natural and historical beauty. You can find attractions that range from ancient ruins to stunning waterfalls, from sandy beaches to mountain peaks, and museums to aquariums. Below are some of the must-see attractions in Antalya, Turkey, for your next visit.

Kaleiçi

This is the old town of Antalya, where you can see the traces of different eras and styles in its architecture. You can visit historical monuments such as Hadrian's Gate, Yivli Minaret Mosque, Hidirlik Tower, and Clock Tower.

You can also stroll around the narrow streets lined with colourful houses, shops, cafes, and bars.

Antalya Museum

This is one of the best museums in Turkey, where you can see a collection of artefacts from various periods and cultures that inhabited Antalya and its surroundings. You can see exhibits such as prehistoric fossils, Roman statues, Byzantine mosaics, Seljuk ceramics, Ottoman weapons, and ethnographic items.

Old Harbor

This is a picturesque harbour in the northwest corner of the old town, where you can see the gently bobbing yachts ready to set out on the Mediterranean. You can also enjoy the views of the sea and the cliffs from the cafes and restaurants on the harbour. You can also hop aboard one of the excursion boats for a day tour catered towards soaking up the sun, taking in the lush coastal views, and swimming in the Mediterranean Sea.

Konyaaltı Beach

This is one of the most popular beaches in Antalya, where you can enjoy the sun, sand, and sea. The beach is about 7 km long and has blue flag status for its cleanliness and facilities. You can find sunbeds, umbrellas, showers, changing rooms, cafes, restaurants, and water sports on the beach.

Düden Waterfalls

These are two spectacular waterfalls located near Antalya. The Upper Düden Waterfall is a 15-meter-high cascade surrounded by a lush park with picnic areas and walking paths. The Lower Düden Waterfall is a 40-meter-high drop that plunges into the Mediterranean Sea from a cliff. You can enjoy the views from a boat or a park on the cliff.

Aspendos

This is an ancient city located about 40 km from Antalya. It is famous for its well-preserved Roman theatre that dates back to the 2nd century AD. The theatre has a capacity of 15,000 people and is still used for concerts and festivals today. You can also see other ruins such as an aqueduct, a basilica, an agora, and a stadium.

Olympos

This is another ancient city located about 80 km from Antalya. It was part of the Lycian League and was known for its natural beauty and piracy activities. You can see ruins such as temples, a theatre, a bathhouse, and a necropolis. You can also enjoy the beach and the nature around the city.

Yanartaş

This is a natural phenomenon located near Olympos. It is a series of flames that burn from the cracks of a rocky hillside. The flames are caused by the emission of methane gas and have been burning for thousands of years. The site is also known as the Chimaera, a mythical fire-breathing creature that was slain by the hero Bellerophon.

Antalya Aquarium

This is one of the largest aquariums in the world, where you can see thousands of marine creatures from different regions and habitats. You can also walk through the world's longest tunnel aquarium, which is 131 meters long and 3 meters wide. You can also enjoy other attractions such as the Snow World, the Ice Museum, the WildPark, and the XD Cinema.

Termessos

This is an ancient city located about 30 km from Antalya. It was one of the most powerful cities of Pisidia, a region in ancient Anatolia. It was also known for its resistance against Alexander the Great in 333 BC. You can see ruins such as a theatre, a gymnasium, an agora, a necropolis, and a fortress.

Tunek Tepe

This is a hill that offers panoramic views of Antalya and its surroundings. You can reach the top by cable car or by road. You can also enjoy a revolving restaurant, a cafe, and a nightclub on the hill.

Lara Beach

This is another popular beach in Antalya, where you can enjoy the sun, sand, and sea. The beach is about 12 km long and has blue flag status for its cleanliness and facilities. You can find sunbeds, umbrellas, showers, changing rooms, cafes, restaurants, and water sports on the beach.

Damlatas Magarasi

This is a cave located near Alanya, about 130 km from Antalya. The cave was discovered in 1948 during the construction of a harbour. It is known for its stalactites and stalagmites that are millions of years old. It is also known for its therapeutic effects on asthma and other respiratory diseases.

These are some of the must-see attractions in Antalya that you can visit during your stay. We hope you have a great time in Antalya!

Recommendations for Accommodation

Below are some recommendations for accommodation in Antalya, based on your preferences and budget:

Villa Mahal in Kalkan: This villa gives a romantic and luxurious feel. It is a whitewashed villa with stunning views of the sea, private pools, a yacht and a restaurant. The price is around $300 per night for a double room.

Deniz Feneri Lighthouse in Kas: If you are looking for a cosy and stylish stay, you may like this hotel with a clever design, spacious rooms, infinity pools, a spa and two restaurants. The price is around $200 per night for a double room.

Ruin Adalia in Antalya Old City: If you are looking for a historical and atmospheric stay, you might like this hotel that consists of five refurbished Ottoman mansions on top of an ancient site, with luxury rooms and suites and a traditional restaurant. The price is around $150 per night for a double room.

Grandpa's Mansion in Finike: If you are looking for a group or family stay, you might like this house that has been converted into two villas that can accommodate four or eight guests, with huge gardens and a barbecue area. The price is around $100 per night for a villa.

Recommendations for Restaurants

Below are some recommendations for restaurants in Antalya, based on your preferences and budget:

Seraser Fine Dining Restaurant in Kaleiçi: If you are looking for a fine dining experience, you might like this restaurant that serves Mediterranean and international cuisine in an elegant and romantic setting. The price is around $50 per person for a three-course meal.

Arma Restaurant in Kaleiçi: If you are looking for a seafood feast, you might like this restaurant that offers fresh fish and seafood dishes with stunning views of the harbour and the mountains. The price is around $30 per person for a main course and a drink.

7 Mehmet in Konyaaltı: If you are looking for a traditional Turkish meal, you might like this restaurant that specializes in kebabs, mezes and desserts from the Antalya region. The price is around $15 per person for a main course and a drink.

Pizza Argentina in Muratpaşa: If you are looking for a pizza treat, you might like this pizzeria that serves authentic Argentinean pizzas with thin crusts and generous toppings. The price is around $10 per person for a pizza and a drink.

Dikkat Et in Muratpaşa: If you are looking for a vegetarian option, you might like this restaurant that serves healthy and delicious dishes made with organic ingredients. The price is around $8 per person for a main course and a drink.

Other Turkey Regions

Turkey is a vast and diverse country that offers a variety of destinations and experiences for travellers. Besides the major cities of Istanbul, Ankara, Bursa, Antalya and Izmir, many other regions are worth exploring and discovering. Below are some of the other regions of Turkey and what they have to offer:

Eastern Anatolia Region: This is the largest and highest region of Turkey, covering most of the Armenian Highlands. It is a land of rugged mountains, volcanic plateaus, deep valleys and glacial lakes. It is also rich in history and culture, as it was home to ancient civilizations such as the Hittites, Urartians, Armenians and Kurds. Some of the attractions in this region include Mount Ararat, the legendary resting place of Noah's Ark, Lake Van, the largest lake in Turkey, Ani, the ruined capital of the medieval Armenian kingdom, and Ishak Pasha Palace, an Ottoman masterpiece of architecture.

Central Anatolia Region: This is the heartland of Turkey, where the Anatolian plateau dominates the landscape. It is a region of steppes, plains, hills and rivers. It is also a region of great historical and cultural significance, as it was the centre of several empires and civilizations, such as the Hittites, Phrygians, Lydians, Persians, Romans, Seljuks and Ottomans. Some of the attractions in this region include Cappadocia, a fairy-tale land of rock formations, cave churches and underground cities, Ankara, the capital and second-largest city of Turkey, Konya, the spiritual home of the whirling dervishes and the poet Rumi, and Hattusa, the ancient capital of the Hittite empire.

Black Sea Region: This is the northernmost region of Turkey, bordering the Black Sea. It is a region of lush green forests, rolling hills, fertile valleys and charming villages. It is also a region of diverse cultures and traditions, influenced by the Greeks, Romans,

Byzantines, Genoese, Ottomans and Russians. Some of the attractions in this region include Trabzon, a historic port city with a Byzantine monastery and a medieval castle, Sumela Monastery, a spectacular cliff-side complex built by Greek monks, Amasya, a picturesque town with Ottoman houses and tombs of Pontic kings, and Safranbolu, a UNESCO World Heritage Site with well-preserved Ottoman architecture.

Mediterranean Region: This is the southernmost region of Turkey, bordering the Mediterranean Sea. It is a region of sunny beaches, turquoise waters, rocky coves and palm trees. It is also a region of ancient history and mythology, as it was part of the classical world of Greece and Rome. Some of the attractions in this region include Antalya, a popular resort city with a historic old town and a Roman harbour, Olympos, an ancient city hidden in a forest by the sea, Aspendos, a Roman city with one of the best-preserved theatres in the world, Perge, another Roman city with impressive ruins and mosaics, and Pamukkale, a natural phenomenon of white travertine terraces filled with mineral-rich water.

Aegean Region: This is the westernmost region of Turkey, bordering the Aegean Sea. It is a region of olive groves, vineyards, islands and bays. It is also a region of legendary history and culture, as it was the cradle of the Trojan War, the Ionian civilization, the Lydian kingdom, and the birthplace of many famous philosophers, poets and scientists. Some of the attractions in this region include Ephesus, one of the best-preserved ancient cities in the world and a UNESCO World Heritage Site, Bodrum, a trendy resort town with a medieval castle and the mausoleum of Halicarnassus, one of the seven wonders of the ancient world, Pergamon, another ancient city that boasts impressive temples and acropolis, and Bergama, a modern town that preserves its Ottoman heritage.

Southeastern Anatolia Region: This is the southeasternmost region of Turkey, bordering Syria and Iraq. It is a region of deserts, mountains, rivers and lakes. It is also a region of diverse ethnicities, religions and languages, such as Turks, Kurds, Arabs, Assyrians, Armenians and Yazidis. Some of the attractions in this region include Gaziantep, a city known for its cuisine, especially baklava, Mardin, a city of stone houses and mosques on a hilltop overlooking the Mesopotamian plain, Diyarbakır, a city with a long history and a massive basalt wall, Urfa, a city of pilgrimage and legends, such as the birthplace of Abraham, and Nemrut

Dağı, a mountain with colossal statues of ancient gods.

Must-see Attractions

Below are some of the must-see attractions in other Turkey regions:

Cappadocia: This is a region in Central Anatolia that is famous for its surreal landscape of fairy chimneys, rock formations, cave churches and underground cities. It is also one of the best places in the world to experience a hot air balloon ride, especially at sunrise or sunset. Some of the attractions in Cappadocia include Göreme

Open-Air Museum, Kaymaklı Underground City, Uçhisar Castle, Paşabağ Valley and Ihlara Valley.

Ephesus: This is an ancient city in the Aegean Region that was once one of the most important and prosperous cities of the Roman Empire. It is home to some of the best-preserved ruins in Turkey, such as the Temple of Artemis, one of the seven wonders of the ancient world, the Library of Celsus, the Great Theater, the Terrace Houses and the Basilica of St. John. Ephesus is also a sacred site for Christians, as it was visited by St. Paul and St. John.

Pamukkale: This is a natural phenomenon in the Aegean Region that consists of white travertine terraces filled with mineral-rich water. The name means "cotton castle" in Turkish, and it is a UNESCO World Heritage Site. Pamukkale is also known for its ancient spa town of Hierapolis, where you can see the ruins of a theatre, a necropolis, a temple and a thermal pool.

Mount Nemrut: This is a mountain in the Southeastern Anatolia Region that is famous for its colossal statues of ancient gods and kings. The statues were built by King Antiochus I of Commagene in the 1st century BCE as part of his royal sanctuary and tomb. The statues are now scattered on the summit and slopes of the mountain, creating a dramatic and mysterious sight. Mount Nemrut is also a UNESCO World Heritage Site.

Patara Beach: This is a beach in the Mediterranean Region that is known for being the longest and one of the most beautiful beaches in Turkey. It stretches for 18 kilometres along the coast, with golden sand and clear blue water. It is also a nesting site for endangered loggerhead turtles and a protected area by law. Patara Beach is also close to the ruins of Patara, an ancient city that was once the capital of Lycia and the birthplace of St. Nicholas.

Recommendations for Accommodation

Below are some recommendations for accommodation in other Turkey regions, based on your preferences and budget:

Liberty Lykia in Fethiye: If you are looking for a wellness retreat, you might like this hotel that offers a range of free activities such as yoga, Pilates, archery and canoeing, as well as a spa and a private beach. The hotel is also situated at the start of the Lycian Way, Turkey's best-known hiking trail. The price is around $200 per night for a double room.

Sundia by Liberty Exclusive in Dalaman: If you are looking for a romantic getaway, you might like this hotel that features tastefully decorated rooms with earthy colours and modern art, as well as infinity pools, a spa and two restaurants. The hotel is also close to Oludeniz, one of the most popular areas with British tourists, where you can paraglide from the Babadag mountain or bathe in the sublime Blue Lagoon. The price is around $150 per night for a double room.

The Courtyard in Kalkan: If you are looking for a historical and atmospheric stay, you might like this guesthouse that consists of two old village houses converted into six bedrooms, with a flower-filled garden and a roof terrace. The guesthouse is located in the heart of the old town of Kalkan, where you can find plenty of restaurants and shops. The price is around $100 per night for a double room.

Club and Hotel Letoonia in Fethiye: If you are looking for a beach-lovers paradise, you might like this hotel that is set on a headland that juts out into the Mediterranean Sea, with three private beaches, four swimming pools and a water park. The hotel also offers various sports and entertainment options, such as tennis, golf, sailing and live shows. The price is around $250 per night for an all-inclusive double room.

Badem Tatil Evi in Selimiye: If you are looking for a cosy and stylish stay, you might like this hotel that offers four simple rooms with lovely views, a small infinity pool and a restaurant that serves superb meze. The hotel is also a short walk from the seaside village of Selimiye, where you can enjoy the tranquil charm and slow pace of life. The price is around $80 per night for a double room.

Recommendations for Restaurants

Below are some recommendations for restaurants in other Turkey regions, based on your preferences and budget:

Seki Restaurant in Cappadocia: If you are looking for a fine dining experience, you might like this restaurant that is located within the world-famous hotel Argos Cappadocia and built inside one of the oldest and largest monasteries in the world. The restaurant serves Mediterranean and international cuisine with local produce, such as slow-cooked meats, artisanal pasta and crispy duck leg. The price is around $50 per person for a three-course meal.

Ferdi Baba Restaurant in Alaçatı: If you are looking for a seafood feast, you might like this restaurant that offers fresh fish and seafood dishes with unique flavours, such as seafood kokoreç, mustard-flavoured anchovies and grilled octopus. The restaurant also has stunning views of the Aegean Sea and delicious desserts such as raspberry or almond-honey souffles. The price is around $30 per person for a main course and a drink.

Çiya Sofrası in Gaziantep: If you are looking for a traditional Turkish meal, you might like this restaurant that specializes in regional dishes from Southeastern Anatolia, such as kebabs, lahmacun, baklava and künefe.

The restaurant also has a rich salad bar with various mezes and pickles. The price is around $15 per person for a main course and a drink.

Pizza Uno in Bodrum: If you are looking for a pizza treat, you might like this pizzeria that serves authentic Italian pizzas with thin crusts and generous toppings. The pizzeria also offers salads, pasta and desserts such as tiramisu and cheesecake. The price is around $10 per person for a pizza and a drink.

Bi Nevi Deli in Cappadocia: If you are looking for a vegetarian option, you might like this restaurant that serves healthy and delicious dishes made with organic ingredients. The restaurant offers soups, salads, wraps, burgers and bowls with various sauces and toppings. The price is around $8 per person for a main course and a drink.

Chapter 5 • Turkish Cuisine and Food Experiences

Introduction to Turkish Cuisine

Turkish cuisine is one of the most diverse and rich cuisines in the world, reflecting the country's long and complex history, geography and culture. Turkish cuisine has been influenced by various culinary traditions from the Mediterranean, Balkan, Middle Eastern, Central Asian and Eastern European regions, as well as by the legacy of the Ottoman Empire, which ruled over many lands and peoples for centuries. Turkish cuisine has also influenced and inspired many other cuisines in its neighbouring countries and beyond.

Turkish cuisine is based on fresh and seasonal ingredients, such as vegetables, fruits, grains, legumes, nuts, dairy products, meat, fish and poultry. Some of the most common ingredients are olive oil, butter, yoghurt, cheese, eggs, honey, bread, rice, bulgur, lentils, chickpeas, beans, olives, tomatoes, cucumbers, peppers, onions, garlic, parsley, mint, dill, oregano, thyme, cumin, paprika, sumac, saffron and sesame seeds. Turkish cuisine also uses a variety of spices and herbs to enhance the flavour and aroma of the dishes.

Turkish cuisine is famous for its variety of soshes and specialities that vary across the country and according to the occasion.

Regional Specialties

Turkish cuisine is not homogeneous but rather varies across the country according to the local climate, geography, culture and history. Each region has its specialities and distinctive flavours that reflect its identity and heritage. Below are some of the regional specialities of Turkish cuisine:

Black Sea Region: This is the northernmost region of Turkey, bordering the Black Sea. It is a region of lush green forests, rolling hills, fertile valleys and charming villages. The cuisine of this region is based on fish, especially anchovies (hamsi), corn, cabbage, kale, hazelnuts and butter. Some of the specialities of this region are hamsili pilav (rice with anchovies), mıhlama (cheese fondue with corn flour), karalahana çorbası (kale soup), kuymak (cheese and cornmeal dish) and laz böreği (custard pastry).

Aegean Region: This is the westernmost region of Turkey, bordering the Aegean Sea. It is a region of olive groves, vineyards, islands and bays. The cuisine of this region is influenced by the Mediterranean and Greek cuisines and is rich in vegetables, herbs, olive oil, cheese, seafood and wine. Some of the specialities of this region are zeytinyağlı yemekler (vegetables cooked in olive oil), ege otları (wild greens), enginar dolması (stuffed artichokes), çipura (sea bream), midye dolma (stuffed mussels) and lokma (fried dough balls).

Marmara Region: This is the northwestern region of Turkey, encompassing Istanbul and its surroundings. It is a region of cultural diversity, cosmopolitanism and sophistication. The cuisine of this region is influenced by the Ottoman palace cuisine, as well as by the Balkan, Armenian, Jewish and European cuisines. Some of the specialities of this region are keşkek (wheat stew with meat), sarma (stuffed grape leaves), börek (stuffed pastry), kuru fasulye (white beans stew), balık ekmek (fish sandwich) and profiterol (cream puffs).

Mediterranean Region: This is the southernmost region of Turkey, bordering the Mediterranean Sea. It is a region of sunny beaches, turquoise waters, rocky coves and palm trees. The cuisine of this region is similar to the Aegean cuisine, but with more spices, meat and citrus fruits. Some of the specialties of this region are Antalya usulü piyaz (bean salad with tahini sauce), Adana kebab (spicy minced meat on skewers), tantuni (meat wrap with tomatoes and parsley), şalgam suyu (turnip juice) and künefe (shredded pastry with cheese and syrup).

Central Anatolia Region: This is the heartland of Turkey, where the Anatolian plateau dominates the landscape. It is a region of steppes, plains, hills and rivers. The cuisine of this region is based on wheat, meat, dairy products, honey and dried fruits. Some of the specialties of this region are mantı (meat dumplings with yoghurt sauce), gözleme (stuffed flatbread), pastırma (cured beef), kaymak (clotted cream), pekmez (grape molasses) and leblebi (roasted chickpeas).

Eastern Anatolia Region: This is the largest and highest region of Turkey, covering most of the Armenian

Highlands. It is a land of rugged mountains, volcanic plateaus, deep valleys and glacial lakes. The cuisine of this region is influenced by the Kurdish, Armenian, Georgian and Iranian cuisines, and is rich in meat, bread, cheese, yogurt and butter. Some of the specialties of this region are cağ kebabı (meat cooked horizontally over a wood fire), erişte (homemade noodles), kete (cheese-filled bread), lor peyniri (ricotta cheese), ayran (yoghurt drink) and baklava (nut-filled pastry with syrup).

Southeastern Anatolia Region: This is the southeasternmost region of Turkey, bordering Syria and Iraq. It is a region of deserts, mountains, rivers and lakes. The cuisine of this region is influenced by the Arab, Persian, Kurdish and Mesopotamian cuisines, and is rich in spices, meat, rice, bulgur, lentils, chickpeas and baklava. Some of the specialties of this region are Urfa kebab (less spicy minced meat on skewers), lahmacun (thin crust of dough topped with minced meat and vegetables), çiğ köfte (raw meatballs), beyran (lamb soup with rice), mütebbel (eggplant dip) and künefe (shredded pastry with cheese and syrup).

Famous Turkish Dishes

Some of the most popular dishes are:

Kebabs: grilled or roasted meat (usually lamb or beef) on skewers or sliced from a vertical spit. There are many types of kebabs in Turkey, such as Adana kebab (spicy minced meat), Urfa kebab (less spicy minced meat), İskender kebab (sliced meat over bread with tomato sauce and yoghurt), Çöp şiş (small pieces of meat on skewers), Şiş tavuk (chicken on skewers) and Cağ kebab (meat cooked horizontally over a wood fire).

Börek: thin layers of pastry (yufka) filled with cheese, spinach, meat or potatoes and baked or fried. There are many types of börek in Turkey, such as su böreği (water börek), sigara böreği (cigar börek), kol böreği (arm börek) and tepsi böreği (tray börek).

Dolma: stuffed vegetables or vine leaves with rice or meat filling. There are many types of dolma in Turkey, such as yaprak dolma (vine leaf dolma), biber dolma (pepper dolma), kabak dolma (zucchini dolma) and lahana dolma (cabbage dolma).

Pilav: rice cooked with butter or oil and sometimes with meat or vegetables. There are many types of pilav in Turkey, such as sade pilav (plain pilav), etli pilav (meat pilav), şehriyeli pilav (vermicelli pilav) and perde pilav (curtain pilav).

Meze: small plates of appetizers or snacks that are served before or along with the main course. There are many types of meze in Turkey, such as haydari (yoghurt with garlic and herbs), çiğ köfte (raw meatballs), patlıcan salatası (eggplant salad), humus (chickpea puree), muhammara (red pepper paste), cacık (yoghurt with cucumber and mint), kısır (bulgur salad), mercimek köftesi (lentil balls) and ezme (spicy tomato salad).

Çorba: soup that is usually served as a starter or a light meal. There are many types of çorba in Turkey, such as mercimek çorbası (lentil soup), tarhana çorbası (fermented wheat soup), ezogelin çorbası (red lentil soup with bulgur and mint), yoğurtlu çorba (yogurt soup), işkembe çorbası (tripe soup) and domates çorbası (tomato soup).

Mantı: small dumplings filled with minced meat or cheese and served with yoghurt and butter sauce. There are many types of mantı in Turkey, such as Kayseri mantısı, çiğ mantı, mantarlı mantı and lahmacun mantısı.

Pide: flatbread topped with cheese, meat, vegetables or eggs and baked in a wood-fired oven. There are many types of pide in Turkey, such as kuşbaşılı pide (meat pide), peynirli pide (cheese pide), karışık pide (mixed pide) and ramazan pidesi (Ramadan pide).

Lahmacun: a thin crust of dough topped with minced meat, onions, parsley and spices and baked in a wood-fired oven. Lahmacun is usually eaten by rolling it up with salad and lemon juice.

Gözleme: stuffed flatbread that is cooked on a griddle. There are many types of gözleme in Turkey, such as peynirli gözleme (cheese gözleme), ıspanaklı gözleme (spinach gözleme), kıymalı gözleme (minced meat gözleme) and patatesli gözleme (potato gözleme).

Baklava: thin layers of pastry (yufka) filled with chopped nuts and soaked in syrup. There are many types of baklava in Turkey, such as fıstıklı baklava (pistachio baklava), cevizli baklava (walnut baklava), kaymaklı baklava (clotted cream baklava) and şöbiyet (baklava with cream and nuts).

Lokum: soft and chewy candy made of starch and sugar and flavored with rose water, lemon, mastic or nuts. Lokum is also known as Turkish delight and is often cut into cubes and dusted with powdered sugar or coconut.

Künefe: shredded pastry (kadayıf) filled with cheese and soaked in syrup. Künefe is usually served hot with clotted cream (kaymak) or ice cream.

Dondurma: Turkish ice cream that is thick and elastic due to the addition of salep (orchid root) and mastic. Dondurma comes in various flavours, such as vanilla, chocolate, pistachio, strawberry and caramel. Dondurma is often sold by street vendors who perform tricks with the ice cream and the long metal rod they use to scoop it. These are just some of the examples of the delicious dishes that Turkish cuisine has to offer. Turkish cuisine is a feast for the senses, a celebration of life and a reflection of the Turkish identity.

Wine and Food Pairing

Turkish cuisine offers a variety of dishes, from grilled meats and kebabs, to stuffed vegetables and pastries, to soups and salads, to desserts and sweets. Turkish cuisine also uses a lot of spices, herbs, yoghurt, cheese, nuts and dried fruits to add flavour and texture to the dishes.

Wine is not traditionally consumed with Turkish food, but some local wines can pair well with different types of Turkish cuisine. Turkey has a long history of wine production, dating back to ancient times, and has several wine regions that produce both indigenous and international grape varieties. Some of the most common Turkish wines are:

Kalecik Karası: This is a red grape variety that produces light-bodied, fruity and floral wines with low tannins and high acidity. It is grown mainly in the Central Anatolia region and can pair well with grilled fish, chicken, lamb or vegetable dishes.

Öküzgözü: This is another red grape variety that produces medium-bodied, spicy and berry-flavoured wines with moderate tannins and acidity. It is grown mainly in the Eastern Anatolia region and can pair well with meaty dishes like kebabs, stews or casseroles.

Narince: This is a white grape variety that produces dry, aromatic and citrusy wines with crisp acidity and mineral notes. It is grown mainly in the Black Sea region and can pair well with seafood, salads, cheese or meze (appetizers).

Emir: This is another white grape variety that produces dry, refreshing and herbal wines with high acidity and floral aromas. It is grown mainly in the Central Anatolia region and can pair well with spicy dishes, soups or pilafs.

Some examples of wine and food pairing in Turkey are:

Pinot Noir with mantı (meat dumplings with yoghurt sauce) or gözleme (stuffed flatbread).

Riesling with hamsili pilav (rice with anchovies) or dolma (stuffed vegetables or vine leaves).

Zinfandel with Adana kebab (spicy minced meat on skewers) or lahmacun (thin crust of dough topped with minced meat and vegetables).

Chardonnay with balık ekmek (fish sandwich) or enginar dolması (stuffed artichokes).

Rosé with börek (stuffed pastry) or kısır (bulgur salad)

Sauternes with baklava (nut-filled pastry with syrup) or lokum (Turkish delight).

Culinary Experiences and Cooking Classes

If you want to learn more about Turkish cuisine and how to prepare some of its delicious dishes, you can join one of the many culinary experiences and cooking classes in Turkey. Below are some of the options you can choose from:

Istanbul Cooking Classes and Food Tours: These classes are held in an Istanbul home and taught in English. Vegetarian, vegan, and gluten-free options are available. The classes include a spice-tasting session, a cooking class and lunch with the food you made, and ferry rides to and from the Asian side of Istanbul.

Cookistan Istanbul Cooking Classes: These classes are taught in either English or German in a private home. The day starts with shopping at small authentic stores and then you head back to cook and chat. The chefs have been cooking for 7 years and are happy to share Turkish traditions and history with you.

Afiyet Olsun Cooking Workshop: This workshop offers more than just a cooking experience. You get picked up from your hotel lobby, take a ferry to the Uskudar area, go to the market to get ingredients, and then meet at the local home to cook with the chef. You are then returned to the hotel unless you ask to see the spice market or other local markets.

Cooking Alaturka: This class teaches you how to make five courses in a class with 2 to 10 people. This class is great for tourists because the chefs are open to talking about what to do and see in the area. The chefs also have more than 16 years of experience and have taught over 5000 classes.

Chapter 6 • Outdoor Activities and Nature

Hiking and Trekking in Turkey

Turkey is a country with diverse and stunning natural beauty, offering many opportunities for hiking and trekking enthusiasts. Whether you prefer coastal views, mountain peaks, ancient ruins or fairy chimneys, you can find a trail that suits your taste and skill level. Below are some of the best hiking and trekking trails in Turkey:

The Lycian Way: One of the most famous hiking trails in Turkey, the Lycian Way stretches around 509km

(316mi) from Fethiye to Antalya, with amazing views all around and great stops along the way, such as Patara Beach, the natural beaches of Kaş and the historic ruins of Olympos. The trail follows the ancient paths of the Lycian civilization and passes through pine forests, rocky cliffs, rural villages and turquoise bays. The trail can be completed in around 25 days, or you can choose to hike shorter sections of it.

Cappadocia: Cappadocia is one of the most unique and magical landscapes in the world, with its surreal rock formations, cave dwellings, underground cities and hot air balloons. Hiking is one of the best ways to explore this wonderland, as many trails take you through the valleys, canyons and hills of Cappadocia. Some of the most popular trails are Pigeon Valley (4km/2.5 mi), Love Valley (5 km/3 mi), Rose Valley (6km/3.7 mi) and Ihlara Valley (14km/8.7 mi).

The Kaçkar Mountains: The Kaçkar Mountains are part of the Pontic Alps in northeastern Turkey, where you can find some of the most challenging and rewarding treks in the country. The mountains are home to glaciers, lakes, waterfalls, alpine meadows and wildlife, as well as traditional villages and monasteries. The highest peak is Kaçkar Dağı at 3,937m (12,917ft), which can be climbed in a two-day round trip from Yaylalar village. Many other trails range from easy to difficult, such as the Trans-Kaçkar Trail (80km/50mi), the Fırtına Valley Trail (40km/25mi) and the Ayder-Yaylalar Trail (18km/11mi).

Cycling in Turkey

Turkey has a well-developed cycling infrastructure that spans the whole country, including the Asian side, which is not very common among other developing countries. Turkey also hosts many cycling competitions and events, making it a popular destination for cyclists of all levels and interests. Below are some of the best cycling routes and tours in Turkey:

The Lycian Way: This is a 509km (316mi) route that follows the ancient paths of the Lycian civilization along the Mediterranean coast from Fethiye to Antalya. The route offers stunning views of the sea, mountains, forests and ruins, as well as charming villages and towns. The route can be completed in around 15 days, or you can choose to cycle shorter sections of it.

Cappadocia: This is one of the most unique and magical regions in the world, with its surreal rock formations, cave dwellings, underground cities and hot air balloons. Cycling is one of the best ways to explore this wonderland, as many trails take you through the valleys, canyons and hills of Cappadocia. Some of the most popular trails are Pigeon Valley (4km/2.5 mi), Love Valley (5 km/3 mi), Rose Valley (6km/3.7 mi) and Ihlara Valley (14km/8.7 mi).

Turkish Thrace: This is the European part of Turkey, where you can find rolling hills, green fields, vineyards and historic towns. Cycling in Turkish Thrace is a great way to experience the rural life and culture of this region, as well as its rich history and heritage. One of the best routes is a 250km (155mi) loop that starts and ends in Istanbul, passing through Edirne, Tekirdağ and Kırklareli.

Watersports in Turkey

Turkey is a country with a long coastline and many inland water bodies, making it an ideal destination for water sports lovers. Whether you are looking for adrenaline or relaxation, you can find a watersport that suits your taste and skill level. Below are some of the best watersports in Turkey:

White water rafting: This is a thrilling sport that involves paddling a raft through rapids and waves on a river. Turkey has many rivers that are suitable for white water rafting, such as Manavgat in Antalya, Fırtına in Rize and Çoruh in Artvin. You can join a guided tour with a professional outfitter and enjoy the scenery and the challenge of this sport.

Windsurfing: This is a sport that combines surfing and sailing, where you use a board with a sail to glide across the water powered by the wind. Turkey has many spots that are ideal for windsurfing, such as Alaçatı in İzmir, Gökova in Muğla and Akyaka in Muğla. You can rent equipment or take lessons from local schools and enjoy the breeze and the waves of this sport.

Kayaking: This is a sport that involves paddling a small boat with a double-bladed paddle on the water. Kayaking is a great way to explore the rocky coastline, the hidden coves and the ancient ruins of Turkey. You can kayak on the sea, such as in Kaş in Antalya, Fethiye in Muğla and Kekova in Antalya, or on the lakes, such as in Eğirdir in Isparta, Bafa in Aydın and Beyşehir in Konya.

Scuba diving: This is a sport that involves diving underwater with a breathing apparatus and exploring marine life and the underwater world. Turkey has many diving sites that offer diverse and colourful reefs, caves, wrecks and fish. Some of the best diving sites are Bodrum in Muğla, Marmaris in Muğla, Antalya in Antalya and Çanakkale in Çanakkale.

Parasailing: This is a sport that involves flying in the air with a parachute attached to a boat. Parasailing is a fun and exhilarating way to enjoy the views of the sea and the land from above. You can parasail in many coastal resorts in Turkey, such as Alanya in Antalya, Kuşadası in Aydın, Marmaris in Muğla and Side in Antalya.

Skiing in Turkey

Skiing in Turkey is a winter activity that can surprise and delight you with its variety, quality and affordability. Turkey has many ski resorts that cater to different levels and preferences of skiers, from beginners to experts, from alpine to cross-country. You can enjoy the snow, the scenery and the culture of this country while skiing in Turkey. Below are some of the best ski resorts in Turkey:

Erciyes – Kayseri: This is the highest ski resort in Turkey, located on Mount Erciyes, a volcanic peak in Central Anatolia. The resort has 55 km (34 mi) of slopes, 14 ski lifts and a snow park. It is suitable for all skill levels and offers panoramic views of the surrounding landscape. The resort is just 40 minutes from Kayseri International Airport and an hour from Cappadocia, a UNESCO World Heritage Site.

Palandöken – Erzurum: This is one of the most popular ski resorts in Turkey, located on Mount Palandöken in Eastern Anatolia. The resort has 43 km (27 mi) of slopes, 13 ski lifts and a heli-skiing service. It is known for its long and challenging runs, as well as its powder snow and sunny weather. The resort is just 30 minutes from Erzurum Airport and close to the historic city of Erzurum, which has many cultural and historical attractions.

Uludağ – Bursa: This is one of the oldest and most famous ski resorts in Turkey, located on Mount Uludağ in the Marmara Region. The resort has 28 km (17 mi) of slopes, 25 ski lifts and a night skiing option. It is suitable for beginners and intermediate skiers, as well as snowboarders and sledders. The resort is just an hour from Bursa Airport and two hours from Istanbul by ferry and car.

Sarıkamış – Kars: This is one of the most unique and scenic ski resorts in Turkey, located on Mount Sarıkamış in Eastern Anatolia. The resort has 21 km (13 mi) of slopes, 5 ski lifts and a cross-country skiing area. It is famous for its crystal snow, which is similar to the snow in the Alps, and its pine forests, which create a fairy-tale atmosphere. The resort is 45 minutes from Kars Airport and close to the ancient city of Ani, a UNESCO World Heritage Site.

Exploring National Parks

Turkey is a country with a rich natural heritage, offering many opportunities for exploring national parks. You can find a national park that suits your interest and taste whether you're looking for wildlife, scenery, history, or culture. Below are some of the best national parks in Turkey:

Beydağları Coastal National Park: This is a national park that covers the Mediterranean coast and the mountains of Antalya province. The park has many attractions, such as the ancient ruins of Olympos and Phaselis, the spectacular beaches of Çıralı and Adrasan, and the mysterious flames of Chimaera. The park is also part of the Lycian Way, a long-distance hiking trail that follows the ancient paths of the Lycian civilization.

Kaçkar Mountains National Park: This is a national park that covers the rugged peaks and valleys of the Kaçkar Mountains in Rize province. The park is a paradise for hikers, trekkers and mountaineers, who can enjoy the glacial lakes, alpine meadows, waterfalls and wildlife of this region. The park is also home to traditional villages and monasteries, where you can experience the local culture and hospitality.

Yedigöller National Park: This is a national park that covers a forested area with seven lakes in Bolu province. The park is a popular destination for nature lovers, who can admire the scenic beauty and tranquillity of this place. The park is especially beautiful in autumn when the leaves change colour and create a stunning contrast with the water. The park is also ideal for camping, fishing, birdwatching and photography.

Göreme National Park: This is a national park that covers an extraordinary landscape of rock formations, cave dwellings, underground cities and churches in Nevşehir province. The park is a UNESCO World Heritage Site and one of the most visited places in Turkey. You can explore the history and culture of this region by visiting the open-air museum, the fairy chimneys, the rock-cut monasteries and the pottery workshops. You can also enjoy a hot air balloon ride over this wonderland at sunrise or sunset.

Beaches and Coastal Escapes

Turkey is a country with a long coastline, offering many options for beaches and coastal escapes. Below are some of the best beaches and coastal escapes in Turkey:

Oludeniz Beach (Blue Lagoon): This is one of the most famous and beautiful beaches in Turkey, located in Fethiye, Dalaman Region. The beach is a natural lagoon with turquoise water, white sand and green hills. It is a popular destination for swimming, sunbathing, paragliding and boat trips.

Kleopatra Beach: This is one of the best beaches in Turkey, located in Alanya, Antalya Region. The beach is named after the Egyptian queen who allegedly bathed here with her lover Mark Antony. The beach has golden sand, clear water and a lively atmosphere. It is a popular destination for water sports, nightlife and sightseeing.

Iztuzu Beach (Turtle Beach): This is one of the most unique and eco-friendly beaches in Turkey, located in Dalyan, Dalaman Region. The beach is a 4.5 km (2.8 mi) long spit of sand that separates the Mediterranean Sea from the Dalyan River. It is a nesting site for the endangered loggerhead turtles, which are protected by conservation efforts. The beach is a popular destination for nature lovers, who can enjoy the scenery, wildlife and boat trips.

Alaçatı Beach: This is one of the most charming and trendy beaches in Turkey, located in Çeşme, Izmir Region. The beach is a former Greek village that has been transformed into a chic resort with stone houses, windmills and bougainvillaea. It is a popular destination for windsurfing, kitesurfing and sailing, as well as shopping, dining and nightlife.

Chapter 7 • Shopping in Turkey

Fashion and Luxury Shopping

Turkey is a country with a vibrant fashion scene, offering many options for fashion and luxury shopping. Below are some of the best places for fashion and luxury shopping in Turkey:

Nişantaşı: This is one of the most upscale and fashionable districts in Istanbul, where you can find luxury boutiques, chic cafes, and elegant architecture. Nişantaşı is home to many international brands, such as

Prada, Gucci, Louis Vuitton, and Marks and Spencer, as well as local designers, such as Arzu Kaprol, Dilek Hanif, and Vakko. You can also visit the City's Nişantaşı Shopping Mall, which has more than 150 stores, restaurants, and cinemas.

Zorlu Center: This is one of the most modern and impressive shopping centres in Istanbul, located in the Beşiktaş district. Zorlu Center has more than 200 stores, including high-end brands, such as Dolce & Gabbana, Burberry, Valentino, and Tiffany & Co., as well as affordable ones, such as H&M, Zara, and Mango. You can also enjoy the cultural and entertainment facilities of Zorlu Center, such as the Performing Arts Center, the Raffles Hotel, and the Cinemaximum Cinema.

Kanyon: This is another stunning shopping centre in Istanbul, located in the Levent district. Kanyon has a unique design that resembles a canyon, with open-air spaces and natural elements. Kanyon has more than 160 stores, including premium brands, such as Harvey Nichols, Michael Kors, Hugo Boss, and Lacoste, as well as local brands, such as Beymen Club, Mavi Jeans, and Hotiç. You can also enjoy the dining and entertainment options of Kanyon, such as the Food Court, the Metrocity Cinema Club, and the Fitness First Gym.

TerraCity: This is one of the largest and most popular shopping centres in Antalya, located in the Lara district. TerraCity has more than 250 stores, including global brands, such as Tommy Hilfiger, Calvin Klein, Guess, and Sephora, as well as Turkish brands, such as İpekyol, Koton, and LC Waikiki. You can also enjoy the leisure and entertainment facilities of TerraCity, such as the FunLab Game Center, the Cinemaximum Cinema Complex, and the Hillside City Club Spa.

Local Markets and Souvenirs

Turkey is a country with a diverse cultural heritage, offering many options for local markets and souvenirs. Below are some of the best local markets and souvenirs in Turkey:

Grand Bazaar: This is one of the oldest and largest covered markets in the world, located in Istanbul. The Grand Bazaar has more than 4000 shops, selling everything from antiques to leather goods, from lamps to carpets, from sweets to spices. You can bargain with the shopkeepers and enjoy the lively atmosphere of this historic market.

Spice Bazaar: This is another famous market in Istanbul, located near the Galata Bridge. The Spice Bazaar is a sensory delight, with colourful and aromatic stalls selling spices, herbs, nuts, dried fruits, teas, coffees, cheeses, and Turkish delights. You can also find souvenirs such as evil eye charms, mosaic lamps, and copperware.

Arasta Bazaar: This is a smaller and quieter market in Istanbul, located behind the Blue Mosque. The Arasta Bazaar has around 70 shops, selling mainly handicrafts, such as carpets, kilims, ceramics, jewellery, and textiles. You can also find a museum of Turkish and Islamic art and a cafe in the bazaar.

Kemeraltı Bazaar: This is a sprawling market in Izmir, located in the city centre. The Kemeraltı Bazaar has hundreds of shops and stalls, selling clothes, shoes, accessories, electronics, books, and more. You can also find historic mosques, synagogues, churches, and caravanserais in the bazaar.

Alaçatı Antika Pazarı: This is a charming market in Alaçatı, a coastal town in Izmir province. The Alaçatı Antika Pazarı is held every Saturday and Sunday in the summer season. The market sells antiques, vintage items, collectables, furniture, art, and more. You can also enjoy the beautiful stone houses, windmills, street art, and cafes of Alaçatı.

Artisan Crafts and Workshops

Turkey offers many options for artisan crafts and workshops. Below are some of the best artisan crafts and workshops in Turkey:

Jewelry Workshop at a Local Studio: This is a workshop that teaches you how to make your jewellery using traditional methods and materials. You can learn from Ayfer, a local jewellery designer and instructor, who will guide you through the process of designing, cutting, soldering, polishing, and engraving your piece of jewellery. You can also visit her studio and see her collection of handmade jewellery.

Pottery Workshop at Avanos: This is a workshop that teaches you how to make your pottery using the clay from the Kızılırmak River. You can learn from the local potters, who have been practising this craft for generations, how to shape, decorate, and fire your pottery. You can also visit the pottery museum and see examples of different styles and techniques of pottery.

Textile Workshop at Safranbolu: This is a workshop that teaches you how to make your textile using natural dyes and fabrics from the region. You can learn from the local women, who have been preserving this craft for centuries, how to dye, weave, embroider, and sew your textile. You can also visit the local bazaar and see the variety of textiles and souvenirs for sale.

Photography Workshop with a National Geographic Photographer: This is a workshop that teaches you how to take stunning photos of Turkey's landscapes, culture, and history. You can learn from Kemal, a professional photojournalist and instructor, who will show you the best spots and angles to capture the beauty of Turkey. You can also get feedback and tips on how to improve your photography skills.

Antique and Vintage Shopping

Whether you are looking for Ottoman relics, Anatolian crafts, European furniture, or retro memorabilia, you can find a shop that sells unique and quality items at various prices. Below are some of the best places for antique and vintage shopping in Turkey:

Grand Bazaar: This is one of the oldest and largest covered markets in the world, located in Istanbul. The Grand Bazaar has more than 4000 shops, selling everything from antiques to leather goods, from lamps to carpets, from sweets to spices. You can bargain with the shopkeepers and enjoy the lively atmosphere of this historic market.

Tellalzade Street: This is one of the main streets for antique shopping on Istanbul's Asian side, located in Kadıköy. Tellalzade Street has many shops and galleries, selling antiques, vintage items, collectables, furniture, art, and more. You can browse through the eclectic displays and find some hidden gems. One of the best shops is Sah Galeri, which sells beautiful vintage furniture, art, porcelain, paintings busts, and more.

Çukurcuma: This is one of the most charming and trendy neighbourhoods in Istanbul, located near Taksim. Çukurcuma has many shops and stalls, selling antiques, vintage items, handicrafts, textiles, jewellery, and more. You can wander through the narrow streets and admire the old houses and street art. Some of the best shops are Aslı Günşiray, which sells high-quality antiques from the Ottoman era and Anatolian art; Modern Tarih, which sells stunning objects from the Far

East; and A la Turca, which sells exclusive antique Anatolian carpets, Ottoman textiles, furniture, pottery, kaftans, ceramics, and more.

Feriköy Flea Market: This is one of the best flea markets in Istanbul, located in Şişli. The Feriköy Flea Market is held every Sunday and attracts many antique seekers who are looking for a good bargain. You can find everything imaginable on this market, such as old photographs, LP records, antique cameras, radios, typewriters, watches, and more. You can also enjoy the local food and drinks at the nearby stalls.

178

Chapter 8 • Practical Information

Health and Safety Tips

Turkey is a fascinating country with stunning natural beauty and delicious cuisine. However, like any destination, it also has some health and safety risks that travellers should be aware of and prepare for. Below are some tips to help you enjoy your trip to Turkey safely and healthily.

Health tips

- Before your trip, check the latest Turkey health advice from the National Travel Health Network and Centre (NaTHNaC) on the TravelHealthPro website. You may need to get some vaccinations or take preventive measures against diseases such as hepatitis A, typhoid, rabies and malaria.
- The European Health Insurance Card (EHIC) and Global Health Insurance Card (GHIC) are not valid in Turkey. Make sure you have adequate travel health insurance and accessible funds to cover the cost of any medical treatment abroad and repatriation.
- Some common prescription and over-the-counter medicines are controlled in Turkey. For more information on controlled medicines and the relevant documentation required, contact the nearest Turkish Embassy or Consulate before you travel.
- British-issued prescriptions are not accepted in pharmacies in Turkey, although some medicines may be available over the counter. If your medical supplies run out while in Turkey, it may be possible, in some cases, to liaise with Turkish

hospitals and your GP to arrange for a Turkish prescription for the equivalent medicine.

- If you need emergency medical assistance during your trip, dial 112 and ask for an ambulance. You should contact your insurance/medical assistance company promptly if you are referred to a medical facility for treatment.

- While travel can be enjoyable, it can sometimes be challenging. There are clear links between mental and physical health, so looking after yourself during travel and when abroad is important.

Safety tips

- You should be vigilant at all times, especially in areas frequented by tourists, such as airports, bus stations, shopping malls, hotels and public transport. Avoid demonstrations and crowds, as they may turn violent or be targeted by terrorists. Follow the advice of local authorities and monitor local media for updates.

- The FCDO advise against all travel to areas within 10km of the border with Syria, due to the recent conflict in Syria and the heightened risk of terrorism in the region. The FCDO also advise against all but essential travel to some provinces in eastern Turkey, such as Sirnak, Hakkari and Agri, where there may be clashes between security forces and Kurdish militants. If you are undertaking essential travel to these areas, you should take extreme care and keep up to date with local developments.

- Crime levels are generally low in Turkey, but street robbery and pick-pocketing are common in the major tourist areas of Istanbul. You should maintain a moderate level of personal security awareness.

- Alcohol and drugs can make you less alert, less in control and less aware of your environment. If you are going to drink, know your limit.

- You should exercise caution when travelling alone or at night, avoid isolated areas and use reputable taxi companies or public transport.

- Turkey is prone to earthquakes, especially in the north-western region near Istanbul and along the Aegean coast. You should familiarise yourself with the safety procedures in case of an earthquake and follow the advice of local authorities.

- Turkey has a hot and dry climate in summer and a cold and wet climate in winter. You should drink plenty of water to avoid dehydration, use sunscreen and wear a hat to protect yourself from sunburn, and dress appropriately for the weather and the local culture. You should also be aware of the risk of heatstroke, especially if you have a pre-existing medical condition or are travelling with children or elderly people. Symptoms of heatstroke include headache, dizziness, nausea, confusion and loss of consciousness. If you or someone you are travelling with shows signs of heatstroke, seek medical attention immediately.

- Turkey has a rich and diverse cuisine that reflects its history and culture. You can enjoy a variety of dishes, such as kebabs, mezes, dolmas, baklava and Turkish delight. However, you should also be careful about food hygiene and avoid eating raw or undercooked meat, eggs, dairy products or seafood. You should also wash your hands before eating and only drink bottled water or boiled water. If you have any food allergies or dietary requirements, you should inform your hotel or restaurant staff before ordering.

We hope these tips help you have a fun and hassle-free trip to Turkey. Enjoy your stay!

Local Laws and Customs

Turkey is a secular republic with a multicultural society. However, it also has some conservative and religious values that may differ from what you're used to. You should respect the local culture and traditions and avoid any behaviour that may cause offence or misunderstanding. Below are some local laws and customs to know before visiting Turkey:

Local laws

- It is illegal not to carry some form of photographic ID in Turkey, such as your passport or driving licence. You may be asked to show your ID by the police or security officials at any time. If you fail to do so, you may face a fine or detention.
- Smoking is illegal on public transport and in all indoor workplaces and public places, such as restaurants, cafes, bars, shopping malls and airports. There are designated smoking areas outside these places. If you smoke in a prohibited area, you may face a fine of up to 900 Turkish Lira.
- The use or possession of some common prescription and over-the-counter medicines is controlled in Turkey. The possession, use or trafficking of illegal drugs is a serious offence in Turkey and can result in a heavy fine, imprisonment or deportation.
- Alcohol is widely available in Turkey, but there are some restrictions on its sale and consumption. You cannot buy alcohol from shops between 10pm and 6am. You cannot drink alcohol in public places, such as parks, streets or

public transport. You cannot drive under the influence of alcohol, as the legal limit is zero.

- Gambling is illegal in Turkey, except for the state-owned lottery and some licensed horse racing venues. You should avoid any forms of gambling, such as online casinos, poker or bingo.
- Homosexuality is not illegal in Turkey, but it is not widely accepted in society. There have been reports of harassment, discrimination and violence against LGBT+ people. You should avoid public displays of affection and be discreet about your sexuality.
- Turkey has strict laws on insulting the Turkish nation, the flag, the president or the founder of the republic, Mustafa Kemal Atatürk. You could face prosecution and imprisonment for expressing opinions that may be considered offensive by the authorities.

Local customs

- Turks greet each other by kissing both cheeks or shaking hands, depending on the level of familiarity and gender. Men usually shake hands with other men, while women may kiss each other on both cheeks. When greeting someone older or more senior than you, you should show respect by slightly bowing your head or kissing their hand.

- The blue eye amulet (nazar boncuğu) is a common symbol in Turkey that is used to ward off evil thoughts or envy. You may see it hanging from cars, houses, jewellery or clothing. It is considered a good luck charm and a friendly gesture to give one as a gift.
- Tea (çay) is a sign of hospitality and friendship in Turkey. You will be offered tea almost everywhere you go, from shops to homes to offices. It is polite to accept at least one glass of tea and drink it slowly while chatting with your host. If you don't want any more tea, place your spoon across the top of your glass or turn it upside down.
- Respect elders by addressing them with formal titles, such as bey (sir), hanım (madam), abi (older brother) or abla (older sister). You should also offer your seat to an elderly person on public transport or at a crowded place.
- Give gold at weddings as a traditional gift for the bride and groom. Gold coins or jewellery are

pinned to the couple's clothes during the wedding ceremony or reception. Alternatively, you can give money in an envelope with your name on it.

- Cover up while visiting a mosque as a sign of respect for the Islamic faith. Men should wear long trousers and shirts with sleeves. Women should wear long skirts or trousers, long-sleeved tops and a headscarf that covers their hair, neck and ears. You should also remove your shoes before entering a mosque and place them in a designated area or carry them in a plastic bag.

- Remove your shoes before entering a home as a sign of cleanliness and courtesy. You may be offered slippers to wear inside the house. You should also avoid stepping on carpets or cushions that are used for sitting or sleeping on the floor.

- Always bring a gift to your host if you are invited to someone's home for a meal or a visit. Suitable gifts include flowers, chocolates, sweets, fruit or wine (if your host drinks alcohol). You should also compliment your host on their home and their food.

Emergency Contacts

Below are some emergency contacts in Turkey that you may need:

You can call 112 for all emergency calls, such as medical, fire, police, coast guard or gendarmerie. The caller is redirected to the appropriate service. Alternatively, you can call the following numbers for specific emergencies:

Fire: 110

Police: 155

Gendarmerie: 156

Coast Guard: 158

Forest Fire: 177

You can call the following numbers for health-related emergencies or consultations:

First Aid: 112

Medical Services and Natural Disasters: 113

Psychological Consultation: 182

Health Consultation: 184

On-duty Pharmacy: 0800 300 001

Emergency Dentistry Service: 0848 261 261

Poisoning Emergency: 145

You can call the following numbers for other useful services:

Telephone Problems: 121

Municipal Police: 153

Traffic Police: 154

Mail: 169

Tourism Police (Istanbul only): (0212) 5274503

Communication and Internet Access

Communication and internet access are essential for travelers who want to stay in touch with their family and friends, share their experiences, or get information about their destination. Turkey is a country with a high level of internet penetration and a variety of options for tourists who want to connect online. Below are some tips on how to get online in Turkey and what to expect from the internet service.

Mobile internet

One of the easiest and most convenient ways to access the internet in Turkey is to use your own smartphone or tablet with a local SIM card. You can buy a SIM card from one of the three main mobile operators in Turkey: Turkcell, Vodafone, or Türk Telekom. You can find their stores at the airport, shopping malls, or city centers. You will need to show your passport and register your device with the operator to activate your SIM card.

You can choose from different prepaid plans that offer data, voice, and SMS services. The prices vary depending on the operator and the package, but you can expect to pay around 100-200 Turkish liras (10-20 US dollars) for a monthly plan with 10-20 GB of data. You can also buy top-ups at convenience stores, kiosks, or ATMs.

The mobile internet coverage and speed are generally good in Turkey, especially in urban areas and tourist destinations. You can use 4G or 5G networks in most places, but you may experience slower or no service in remote or rural areas. You can also use your phone as a hotspot to share your internet connection with other devices.

Wi-Fi

Another option to access the internet in Turkey is to use Wi-Fi networks that are available in many public places, such as hotels, cafes, restaurants, museums, parks, or shopping centers. You can usually connect to these networks for free or for a small fee, but you may need to ask for a password or register with your phone number or email address.

The Wi-Fi quality and speed may vary depending on the location and the number of users. Some Wi-Fi networks may be unreliable, slow, or insecure, so you should avoid using them for sensitive tasks such as banking or shopping online. You should also use a VPN (virtual private network) service to protect your privacy and security when using public Wi-Fi networks.

Internet cafes

If you don't have a mobile device or you need to use a computer for some reason, you can also visit an internet cafe in Turkey. Internet cafes are common in big cities and tourist areas, and they usually charge by the hour or by the minute. You can use their computers to browse the web, check your email, print documents, or play games.

The internet cafes are usually open until late at night or 24 hours a day. They may also offer other services such as scanning, copying, faxing, or phone calls. The internet speed and quality may vary depending on the cafe and the time of day. You should also be careful about your personal information and log out of any accounts when you finish using the computer.

Some cultural tips

When communicating online in Turkey, you should be aware of some cultural norms and etiquette that may differ from your own country. Here are some tips to help you avoid misunderstandings or offense:

Turkish people are generally very friendly and warm online, and they may use emojis, stickers, gifs, or voice messages to express their emotions.

Turkish people may also use informal language, abbreviations, slang, or jokes when chatting online, especially with their friends or family.

Turkish people may also use honourifics such as abi (older brother), abla (older sister), bey (sir), hanım (madam), hocam (teacher), or doktorum (doctor) when addressing someone online.

Turkish people may also use terms of endearment such as canım (my soul), tatlım (my sweet), hayatım (my life), or güzelim (my beautiful) when talking to someone they like online.

Turkish people may also use compliments such as çok güzelsin (you are very beautiful), çok yakışıklısın (you are very handsome), çok zekisin (you are very smart), or çok başarılısın (you are very successful) when praising someone online.

Turkish people may also use questions such as naber? (what's up?), nasılsın? (how are you?), ne yapıyorsun? (what are you doing?), nereye gidiyorsun? (where are you going?), ne zaman görüşeceğiz? (when will we see each other?), or ne istiyorsun? (what do you want?) when starting a conversation online.

Turkish people may also use expressions such as inşallah (God willing), maşallah (God has willed it), hayırlı olsun (may it be good), geçmiş olsun (get well soon), or kolay gelsin (may it be easy) when wishing someone well online.

We hope this guide has given you some useful information on how to access and use the internet in Turkey.

Chapter 9 • Recommended Itineraries

Aegean Adventure Itinerary: Istanbul, Gallipoli, Troy, Pergamum, Ephesus, Pamukkale in 7 days

If you're looking for an adventure that combines history, culture, and nature, then this 7-day itinerary is perfect for you. You'll explore the highlights of the Aegean coast, from the cosmopolitan Istanbul to the ancient ruins of Troy, Pergamum, and Ephesus. You'll also visit the poignant battlefields of Gallipoli, the stunning white terraces of Pamukkale, and the thermal springs of Hierapolis. Along the way, you'll enjoy delicious Turkish cuisine, shop for souvenirs in colorful bazaars, and experience the hospitality of the local people.

Day 1: Istanbul

Arrive in Istanbul, the largest city and former capital of Turkey, and transfer to your hotel. Depending on your arrival time, you can start exploring this fascinating city that straddles two continents: Europe and Asia. You can visit some of the iconic landmarks, such as the Hagia Sophia, the Blue Mosque, the Topkapi Palace, and the Grand Bazaar. You can also take a cruise on the Bosphorus Strait, which offers stunning views of the city skyline and the bridges that connect the two sides. In the evening, you can enjoy a traditional Turkish dinner and a show featuring belly dancers and folk music.

Day 2: Gallipoli

After breakfast, depart from Istanbul and drive to Gallipoli, where one of the most famous battles of World War I took place. Here, you'll visit the memorials and cemeteries that commemorate the thousands of Turkish and Allied soldiers who lost their lives in this tragic campaign. You'll also see some of the key sites of the battlefields, such as Anzac Cove, Lone Pine, Chunuk Bair, and The Nek. You'll learn about the history and significance of this event that shaped the national identity of both Turkey and Australia. After a full day of touring, you'll check into your hotel in Canakkale.

Day 3: Troy - Pergamum - Kusadasi

After breakfast, drive to Troy, the legendary city where the Trojan War took place. Here, you'll see the archaeological remains of this ancient civilization that dates back to 3000 BC. You'll also see a replica of the wooden horse that was used by the Greeks to enter the city and end the 10-year siege. Next, drive to Pergamum, another ancient city that was once a powerful kingdom and a center of culture and learning. Here, you'll visit the Acropolis, which features impressive temples, palaces, and theatres. You'll also see the Asclepion, which was one of the first medical centers in history. After a day of exploring these ancient wonders, you'll continue to Kusadasi, a popular resort town on the Aegean coast.

Day 4: Ephesus

After breakfast, drive to Ephesus, one of the best-preserved ancient cities in the world. Here, you'll walk along the marble streets and admire the magnificent buildings that reflect the glory of this former Roman capital. You'll see the Library of Celsus, which was one of the largest libraries in antiquity; the Temple of Artemis, which was one of the Seven Wonders of the Ancient World; the Theatre, which could seat 25,000 spectators; and many more. You'll also visit the House of Virgin Mary, where it is believed that Mary spent her last years after fleeing Jerusalem with Saint John. After a full day of touring this amazing site, you'll return to your hotel in Kusadasi.

Day 5: Pamukkale - Hierapolis

After breakfast, drive to Pamukkale, which means "cotton castle" in Turkish. Here, you'll see one of the most spectacular natural phenomena in Turkey: a series of white limestone terraces that cascade down a hillside like a frozen waterfall. These terraces are formed by mineral-rich hot springs that flow over them and create pools of turquoise water. You can walk on these terraces or soak in these pools and enjoy their therapeutic benefits. Next to Pamukkale is Hierapolis, an ancient city that was founded as a spa and a healing center.

Here, you'll see the ruins of temples, baths, tombs, and a theatre. You'll also see the Necropolis, which is one of the largest and most diverse cemeteries in the ancient world. After a day of marveling at these natural and man-made wonders, you'll check into your hotel in Pamukkale.

Day 6: Pamukkale - Istanbul

After breakfast, drive back to Istanbul, stopping along the way to enjoy the scenic views of the countryside. You'll arrive in Istanbul in the evening and check into your hotel. You can spend the rest of the day at your leisure, exploring more of this vibrant city or relaxing in your hotel.

Day 7: Istanbul - Departure

After breakfast, transfer to the airport for your flight back home or to your next destination. You'll leave Turkey with unforgettable memories and experiences of this amazing Aegean adventure.

Beaches & Ruins of the Turquoise Coast: Antalya, Kas, Kalkan, Fethiye in 7 days

If you're looking for a beach holiday with a twist, then this 7-day itinerary is ideal for you. You'll discover the beauty and diversity of Turkey's Turquoise Coast, a stretch of coastline that boasts turquoise waters, golden sands, and ancient ruins. You'll also enjoy the culture and cuisine of this region, which blends Mediterranean, Anatolian, and Lycian influences. Here's how to make the most of your time on the Turquoise Coast.

Day 1: Antalya

Arrive in Antalya, the largest city and gateway to the Turquoise Coast, and transfer to your hotel. Depending on your arrival time, you can start exploring this lively city that combines modern amenities with historic charm. You can visit the old town of Kaleiçi, where you'll find narrow streets, Ottoman houses, and Roman monuments. You can also visit the Antalya Museum, which displays artifacts from the region's rich history and culture. In the evening, you can enjoy a delicious meal at one of the many restaurants that offer fresh seafood, kebabs, mezes, and more.

Day 2: Olympos - Adrasan

After breakfast, drive to Olympos, an ancient city that was once a pirate stronghold and a center of worship for the god of fire. Here, you'll see the ruins of temples, theatres, baths, and tombs that are scattered among the pine trees and the beach. You'll also see the eternal flames of Chimaera, a natural phenomenon that produces fire from cracks in the rocks. Next, drive to Adrasan, a tranquil bay with a long sandy beach and clear water. Here, you can relax on the beach or enjoy some water sports such as kayaking, snorkeling, or diving.

Day 3: Kekova - Kaş

After breakfast, drive to Kekova, a stunning area that features a sunken city, an island, and a castle. Here, you can take a boat tour to see the underwater ruins of an ancient town that was destroyed by an earthquake. You can also visit the island of Kekova, where you'll find more ruins and a charming fishing village. You can also visit the castle of Simena, which offers panoramic views of the bay and the sea. Next, drive to Kaş, a charming town that is popular with travelers and locals alike. Here, you can stroll along the harbor, shop at the boutiques and bazaars, or enjoy a drink at one of the cafes and bars.

Day 4: Patara - Kalkan

After breakfast, drive to Patara, one of the longest and most beautiful beaches in Turkey. Here, you can sunbathe on the soft sand or swim in the warm sea. You can also visit the ancient site of Patara, which was once a major port and the birthplace of Saint Nicholas. Here, you'll see the remains of a lighthouse, a theatre, a parliament building, and a necropolis. Next, drive to Kalkan, a picturesque town that is perched on a hill overlooking the sea. Here, you can enjoy the views of the bay and the islands, or explore the old town with its whitewashed houses and colorful flowers. You can also dine at one of the rooftop restaurants that offer delicious Turkish and international cuisine.

Day 5: Fethiye

After breakfast, drive to Fethiye, a bustling town that is surrounded by mountains and lagoons. Here, you can visit the Lycian rock tombs that are carved into the cliffs, or the Fethiye Museum that showcases the history and culture of the region. You can also take a boat trip to the nearby islands, such as Gemiler Island, where you'll find Byzantine ruins and a church. Or you can visit the Butterfly Valley, a secluded cove that is home to hundreds of butterflies.

Day 6: Ölüdeniz - Kayaköy

After breakfast, drive to Ölüdeniz, one of the most famous and photographed beaches in Turkey. Here, you'll see the blue lagoon that is surrounded by pine forests and mountains. You can relax on the beach or swim in the crystal-clear water. You can also try some adventure sports such as paragliding, which will give you a bird's-eye view of the stunning scenery. Next, drive to Kayaköy, a ghost town that was once inhabited by Greek Christians who were forced to leave after the population exchange of 1923. Here, you'll see the abandoned houses, churches, and schools that are still standing as a reminder of the past.

Day 7: Dalaman - Departure

After breakfast, drive to Dalaman airport for your flight back home or to your next destination. You'll leave Turkey with unforgettable memories and experiences of this beautiful and diverse Turquoise Coast.

Capitals of Empire: Istanbul, Bursa, Iznik in 7 days

If you're interested in the history and culture of the Ottoman Empire, then this 7-day itinerary is perfect for you. You'll visit three cities that served as capitals for the Ottomans at different times: Istanbul, Bursa, and Iznik. You'll see the magnificent monuments, mosques, palaces, and tombs that reflect the glory and diversity of this empire that spanned six centuries and three continents. You'll also enjoy the natural beauty, cuisine, and crafts of these regions, which blend Turkish, Islamic, Byzantine, and Anatolian influences. Here's how to make the most of your time in the capitals of the Ottoman Empire.

Day 1: Istanbul

Arrive in Istanbul, the largest city and the final capital of the Ottoman Empire, and transfer to your hotel. Depending on your arrival time, you can start exploring this fascinating city that straddles two continents: Europe and Asia. You can visit some of the iconic landmarks that were built by the Ottoman sultans, such as the Topkapi Palace, the Blue Mosque, the Suleymaniye Mosque, and the Grand Bazaar. You can also visit some of the earlier Byzantine monuments that were converted by the Ottomans, such as the Hagia Sophia and the Chora Church. In the evening, you can enjoy a traditional Turkish dinner and a show featuring whirling dervishes and folk music.

Day 2: Bursa

After breakfast, depart from Istanbul and take a ferry across the Sea of Marmara to Bursa, the first capital of the Ottoman Empire. Here, you'll see the tombs of

Osman I and Orhan I, the founders of the Ottoman dynasty, as well as other sultans and princes. You'll also see some of the finest examples of Ottoman architecture, such as the Ulu Mosque, the Green Mosque, and the Green Tomb. You'll also visit the Koza Han, a historic caravanserai that is famous for its silk production and trade. You can shop for silk scarves, carpets, and other souvenirs at the nearby bazaar. After a full day of touring, you'll check into your hotel in Bursa.

Day 3: Iznik

After breakfast, drive to Iznik, formerly known as Nicaea, an ancient city that was once a capital of both the Byzantine and Ottoman empires. Here, you'll see the ruins of Roman walls, gates, aqueducts, and baths that date back to the 1st century AD. You'll also see some of the most important churches in Christian history, such as the Hagia Sophia and the Church of St. Mary (also known as St. Tryphon), where two ecumenical councils were held in 325 and 787 AD. You'll also see some of the finest examples of Ottoman tile work, such as the Yesil Mosque and the Nilufer Hatun Imaret. You can also visit a tile workshop and learn how to make your own ceramic art. After a day of exploring this historic city, you'll drive back to Bursa and spend the night at your hotel.

Day 4: Istanbul

After breakfast, drive back to Istanbul and check into your hotel. You can spend the rest of the day at your leisure, exploring more of this vibrant city or relaxing in your hotel. You can also take a cruise on the Bosphorus Strait, which offers stunning views of the city skyline and the bridges that connect the two sides. You can also visit some of the museums that showcase the history and culture of the Ottoman Empire, such as the Istanbul Archaeological Museum, the Turkish and Islamic Arts Museum, and the Museum of Turkish and Islamic Calligraphy.

Day 5: Edirne

After breakfast, depart from Istanbul and drive to Edirne, the second capital of the Ottoman Empire. Here, you'll see some of the most impressive monuments that were built by the Ottoman sultans, such as the Selimiye Mosque, which is considered to be the masterpiece of the architect Sinan. You'll also see the Eski Mosque, the Uc Serefeli Mosque, and the Beyazit II Complex, which includes a mosque, a hospital, a medical school, and a soup kitchen. You'll also visit the Edirne Palace, which was once the largest and most splendid palace in the Ottoman Empire. After a full day of touring, you'll check into your hotel in Edirne.

Day 6: Istanbul

After breakfast, drive back to Istanbul and check into your hotel. You can spend the rest of the day at your leisure, exploring more of this vibrant city or relaxing in your hotel. You can also visit some of the other attractions that Istanbul has to offer, such as the Dolmabahce Palace, which was the last residence of the Ottoman sultans; the Spice Bazaar, which is filled with exotic aromas and flavors; or the Galata Tower, which offers panoramic views of the city.

Day 7: Istanbul - Departure

After breakfast, transfer to the airport for your flight back home or to your next destination. You'll leave Turkey with unforgettable memories and experiences of this amazing journey through the capitals of the Ottoman Empire.

Cappadocia Itinerary: Goreme Open Air Museum, Ihlara Valley in 2-3 days

Cappadocia is a magical region in central Turkey that is famous for its fairy chimneys, rock-cut churches, underground cities, and hot air balloon rides. With 2-3 days in Cappadocia, you can experience the best of this unique landscape and culture. Here's a suggested itinerary for your Cappadocia trip.

Day 1: Goreme Open Air Museum, Sword Valley, Rose Valley

Start your day by visiting the Goreme Open Air Museum, a UNESCO World Heritage site that showcases the monastic life and art of the Byzantine era. Here, you can see several rock-cut churches, chapels, and monasteries that are decorated with colorful frescoes depicting biblical scenes. Some of the highlights include the Dark Church, the Apple Church, and the Chapel of St. Barbara.

Next, take a short walk to the Sword Valley, a narrow valley that is named after the sword-shaped rock formations that rise from the ground. Here, you can enjoy the views of the fairy chimneys and the Uchisar Castle, the highest point in Cappadocia. You can also explore some of the caves and tunnels that were used by the locals as shelters and storage.

Continue your walk to the Rose Valley, one of the most beautiful valleys in Cappadocia. Here, you can see different shades of pink and red on the rocks, especially at sunset. You can also see some of the most impressive rock-cut churches in Cappadocia, such as the Church of Three Crosses, the Church of Columns, and the Church of St. John.

In the evening, you can choose to join a horse riding or an ATV tour that will take you to some of the hidden spots and viewpoints in Cappadocia. You can also enjoy a traditional Turkish dinner and a show featuring folk dances and music.

Day 2: Ihlara Valley, Selime Cathedral, Kaymakli Underground City

On your second day, you can join a guided tour that will take you to some of the most interesting sites in Cappadocia. The first stop is the Ihlara Valley, a 14-km-long gorge that was formed by a volcanic eruption and carved by a river. Here, you can hike along the river and see more than 100 rock-cut churches and monasteries that are hidden among the trees and cliffs. Some of the most notable ones are the Agacalti Church, the Yilanli Church, and the Kokar Church.

Next, visit the Selime Cathedral, a huge complex of rock-cut structures that was once a religious center and a fortress. Here, you can see a cathedral, a monastery, a mosque, a kitchen, a stable, and several rooms that are connected by stairs and tunnels. You can also admire the intricate carvings and paintings on the walls and ceilings.

The last stop is the Kaymakli Underground City, one of the largest and most impressive underground cities in Cappadocia. Here, you can explore some of the eight levels that were dug by the ancient people as a refuge from invaders and natural disasters. You can see how they lived, worked, worshiped, and defended themselves in this subterranean world. You can see ventilation shafts, storage rooms, kitchens, wine cellars, churches, and even a school.

Day 3: Pigeon Valley, Uchisar Castle, Love Valley
On your third day, you can explore some of the other valleys and viewpoints in Cappadocia. Start with the Pigeon Valley, a scenic valley that is named after the pigeon houses that are carved into the rocks. Here, you can see how the locals used to collect pigeon droppings as fertilizer for their crops. You can also enjoy the views of the fairy chimneys and the orchards.

Next, visit the Uchisar Castle, a massive rock formation that was used as a fortress and a lookout point by the locals. Here, you can climb to the top and enjoy the panoramic views of Cappadocia. You can also see some of the rooms and windows that are carved into the rock.

Finally, visit the Love Valley, another valley that is famous for its phallic-shaped fairy chimneys. Here, you can have some fun taking photos and making jokes about these unusual rock formations. You can also see some of the caves and churches that are hidden among the rocks.

In the evening, you can catch your flight back to Istanbul or to your next destination. You'll leave Cappadocia with unforgettable memories and experiences of this magical region.

Exploring the Southeast of Turkey: Mount Nemrut, Sanliurfa in 4-5 days

The southeast of Turkey is a region rich in history, culture, and natural beauty. With 4-5 days, you can explore some of the highlights of this area, such as

Mount Nemrut, Sanliurfa, and Harran. Here's a suggested itinerary for your trip.

Day 1: Mount Nemrut

Start your day by driving to Mount Nemrut, a UNESCO World Heritage site that features a colossal funerary monument of King Antiochus I of the Kingdom of Commagene. Here, you can see the huge statues of gods and kings that surround the artificial mound that covers the king's tomb. The statues have lost their heads, which now lie on the ground, creating a surreal and impressive sight. You can also see the reliefs and inscriptions that depict the king's ancestry and beliefs.

The best time to visit Mount Nemrut is at sunrise or sunset, when the light creates a dramatic effect on the statues and the surrounding landscape. You can also see the Lion Horoscope, a stone slab that shows the arrangement of stars and planets on the day of the monument's inauguration in 62 BC.

After visiting Mount Nemrut, you can drive to Kahta or Adiyaman and spend the night there.

Day 2: Sanliurfa

After breakfast, drive to Sanliurfa, a city that is considered to be one of the oldest and most sacred places in the world. Here, you can visit the Balikli Gol

(Fish Lake), where according to legend, Abraham was thrown into a fire by Nimrod, but God turned the fire into water and the coals into fish. You can also see the Halil Rahman Mosque and the Rizvaniye Mosque that flank the lake.

Next, visit the Sanliurfa Museum, which displays artifacts from various periods of history, such as Neolithic, Chalcolithic, Bronze Age, Iron Age, Roman, Byzantine, Islamic, and Ottoman. You can also see the Gobeklitepe Hall, which showcases replicas of the stone pillars and sculptures from Gobeklitepe, an archaeological site that is believed to be the oldest temple in the world.

In the afternoon, you can stroll around the old town of Sanliurfa and see the traditional houses, bazaars, and cafes. You can also visit the Sanliurfa Castle, which offers panoramic views of the city.

Day 3: Gobeklitepe - Harran

After breakfast, drive to Gobeklitepe, a UNESCO World Heritage site that is located about 15 km from Sanliurfa. Here, you can see the remains of a complex of circular and oval-shaped structures that date back to the 10th millennium BC. The structures are made of massive stone pillars that are carved with animal and human figures. The site is considered to be the oldest temple in the world and a major discovery for the understanding of human history and civilization.

Next, drive to Harran, a town that has a history of more than 6,000 years. Here, you can see the distinctive beehive-shaped houses that are made of mud bricks and have conical roofs. You can also see the ruins of the Harran University, which was one of the first Islamic universities in the world and a center of science and culture. You can also see the Harran Grand Mosque, which was built in the 8th century and is one of the oldest mosques in Turkey.

After visiting Harran, you can drive back to Sanliurfa and spend the night there.

Day 4: Halfeti - Gaziantep

After breakfast, drive to Halfeti, a town that is partially submerged under water due to the construction of a dam. Here, you can take a boat tour on the Euphrates River and see the sunken houses, mosques, and bridges. You can also see the Rumkale Fortress, which is located on a rocky island and was once a strategic point for various civilizations. You can also visit the village of Savasan Koyu (Drowned Village), where you can see the minaret of a mosque sticking out of the water.

Next, drive to Gaziantep, a city that is famous for its cuisine, especially its baklava (a sweet pastry with nuts and syrup). Here, you can visit the Gaziantep Museum of Archaeology, which displays artifacts from various periods of history, such as Hittite, Assyrian, Babylonian, Persian, Greek, Roman, Byzantine, Seljuk, Mongol, Ottoman, and Turkish. You can also visit the Gaziantep Zeugma Mosaic Museum, which showcases stunning mosaics from the ancient city of Zeugma that was located on the Euphrates River.

In the evening, you can enjoy a delicious meal at one of the many restaurants that offer local specialties such as kebabs, lahmacun (a thin crust pizza with minced meat and vegetables), pistachio baklava, and katmer (a flaky pastry with pistachio and cream).

Day 5: Departure

After breakfast, transfer to the airport for your flight back home or to your next destination. You'll leave Turkey with unforgettable memories and experiences of this amazing region.

Southern Mediterranean: Side Town, Aspendos Theatre in 7 days

The southern Mediterranean coast of Turkey is a region of stunning natural beauty and cultural heritage. With 7 days, you can explore some of the highlights of this area, such as Side, Aspendos, and Manavgat. Here's a suggested itinerary for your trip.

Day 1: Antalya

Arrive in Antalya, the largest city and the gateway to the southern Mediterranean coast, and transfer to your hotel. Depending on your arrival time, you can start exploring this lively city that combines modern amenities with historic charm. You can visit the old town of Kaleici, where you'll find narrow streets, Ottoman houses, and Roman monuments. You can also visit the Antalya Museum, which displays artifacts from the region's rich history and culture. In the evening, you can enjoy a delicious meal at one of the many restaurants that offer fresh seafood, kebabs, mezes, and more.

Day 2: Aspendos - Manavgat

After breakfast, depart from Antalya and drive to Aspendos, an ancient city that is famous for its well-preserved Roman theater. Here, you can see the theater that was built in the 2nd century AD and could seat up to 15,000 people. The theater is still used for concerts and performances to this day. You can also see the ruins of other buildings, such as the aqueduct, the basilica, the stadium, and the agora.

Next, drive to Manavgat, a town that is known for its scenic waterfall. Here, you can see the waterfall that cascades over a rocky cliff into a pool of blue water. You can also enjoy a boat ride on the Manavgat River or visit the nearby bazaar. After visiting Manavgat, drive back to Antalya and spend the night there.

Day 3: Side

After breakfast, drive to Side, an ancient port city that was once a center of trade and culture. Here, you can see the impressive ruins of temples, theaters, baths, and tombs that date back to the Greek and Roman periods. You can also see the museum that is housed in a former Roman bath and displays statues and mosaics from the site. You can also visit the harbor, where you'll find cafes, shops, and boats.

Side is also famous for its beautiful beaches, where you can relax on the golden sand or swim in the turquoise sea. You can also enjoy some water sports such as parasailing, jet skiing, or diving.

Day 4: Alanya

After breakfast, drive to Alanya, a popular resort town that is located on a peninsula. Here, you can visit the Alanya Castle, a medieval fortress that overlooks the town and the sea. You can also see the Red Tower, a defensive tower that was built by the Seljuks in the 13th century. You can also visit the Damlatas Cave, a natural cave that is famous for its stalactites and stalagmites.

Alanya also has many beaches, where you can enjoy the sun and the sea. You can also visit the Cleopatra Beach, which is said to be where the Egyptian queen bathed during her visit to Alanya. You can also visit the Dim Cayi, a river that flows through a canyon and offers a refreshing escape from the heat. In the evening, you can enjoy the nightlife of Alanya.

Day 5: Anamur - Silifke

After breakfast, depart from Alanya and drive along the coast to Anamur, a town that is home to one of the best-preserved Roman castles in Turkey. Here, you can see the Anamurium Castle, which was built in the 3rd century AD and covers an area of 25 hectares. You can also see the ruins of an ancient city that was once a prosperous port and trade center. You can also visit the Mamure Castle, which was built by the Crusaders in the 13th century and later expanded by the Ottomans.

Next, drive to Silifke, a town that has a history of more than 3,000 years. Here, you can see the Silifke Castle, which was built by the Byzantines in the 7th century and later used by the Crusaders and the Ottomans. You can also see the ruins of Seleucia ad Calycadnum, an ancient city that was founded by Alexander the Great's general Seleucus I Nicator. You can also visit the Cennet ve

Cehennem (Heaven and Hell), two natural sinkholes that are connected by an underground cave. After visiting Silifke, drive to Mersin and spend the night there.

Day 6: Tarsus - Adana

After breakfast, drive to Tarsus, a city that is famous for being the birthplace of St. Paul, one of the apostles of Christianity. Here, you can see the St. Paul's Well, where according to legend, St. Paul drank water from during his visit to Tarsus. You can also see the St. Paul's Church, which was built on the site of his house. You can also see the Cleopatra's Gate, which is said to be where Cleopatra entered Tarsus to meet Mark Antony.

Next, drive to Adana, a city that is known for its cuisine, especially its spicy kebab. Here, you can visit the Adana Archaeological Museum, which displays artifacts from various periods of history, such as Hittite, Assyrian, Roman, Byzantine, Seljuk, Mongol, Ottoman, and Turkish. You can also visit the Sabanci Central Mosque, which is the largest mosque in Turkey and one of the largest in the world. You can also visit the Stone Bridge, which is the oldest bridge in the world that is still in use. You can also visit the Taskopru, a Roman bridge that was built by Emperor Hadrian. In the evening, you can enjoy a delicious meal of Adana kebab and other local specialties.

Day 7: Departure

After breakfast, transfer to the airport for your flight back home or to your next destination. You'll leave Turkey with unforgettable memories and experiences of this amazing region.

Chapter 10 • Travelling with Children

Family-Friendly Attractions

Turkey is a wonderful destination for families, as it offers a variety of attractions and activities that cater to different ages and interests. Below are some of the best family-friendly attractions in Turkey that you should not miss.

Istanbul

Istanbul is the largest and most vibrant city in Turkey, and it has plenty of attractions to keep your family entertained. You can visit some of the iconic landmarks of Istanbul, such as the Blue Mosque, Hagia Sophia, Topkapi Palace, and Basilica Cistern, and learn about their fascinating history and architecture. You can also take a cruise along the Bosphorus Strait, which separates Europe and Asia, and enjoy the scenic views of the city and its surroundings. For some fun and education, you can visit the Istanbul Aquarium, which has more than 15,000 marine creatures from different regions of the world, or the Legoland Discovery Centre, which has interactive exhibits and rides for kids. If you are looking for some thrill and excitement, you can head to Vialand Theme Park, which has roller coasters, water slides, 4D cinema, and more.

Cappadocia

Cappadocia is an area of Turkey that is known for its unique landscape, formed by volcanic eruptions and erosion over millions of years. The result is a stunning scenery of fairy chimneys, rock formations, caves, and valleys that look like something out of a fantasy movie. Cappadocia is a great place to go hiking, horseback riding, or biking with your family, as you can explore the natural beauty and discover the ancient churches and villages carved into the rocks. The highlight of

Cappadocia, however, is the hot air balloon ride that takes you over the surreal landscape at sunrise or sunset. This is an unforgettable experience that will leave you breathless and amazed.

Pamukkale

Pamukkale is another natural wonder of Turkey that is worth visiting with your family. Pamukkale means "cotton castle" in Turkish, and it refers to the white terraces of travertine pools that cascade down the hillside. These pools are filled with mineral-rich water that has therapeutic properties and a pleasant temperature. You can swim or soak in these pools with your family and enjoy the relaxing and healing effects. You can also visit the nearby ancient city of Hierapolis, which was a spa center in Roman times and has ruins of temples, baths, theaters, and tombs.

Fethiye

Fethiye is a coastal town in southwestern Turkey that is popular for its beaches, resorts, and water sports. You can find some of the best beaches in Turkey in Fethiye, such as Oludeniz Beach, which has a blue lagoon and a paragliding spot; Calis Beach, which has a long promenade and a sunset view; or Butterfly Valley Beach, which has a secluded cove and a waterfall. You can also enjoy activities like snorkeling, diving, kayaking, sailing, or fishing with your family in Fethiye. If you want to explore more of the region's culture and nature, you can visit some of the nearby attractions like Kayakoy Ghost Town, which is an abandoned Greek village; Saklikent Gorge, which is a deep canyon with a river; or Tlos Ancient City, which is one of the oldest settlements in Lycia.

Child-Friendly Accommodation

Turkey has a wide range of accommodation options for families, from luxury resorts and hotels to cozy apartments and villas. You can find child-friendly facilities and services such as swimming pools, playgrounds, kids clubs, babysitting, and family rooms in many places. Below are some of the best child-friendly accommodation in Turkey that you can choose from.

Hotels

Hotels are a convenient and comfortable choice for families, as they offer amenities such as breakfast, cleaning, and security. You can also enjoy the on-site facilities such as restaurants, bars, spas, and gyms. Some hotels also have water parks, splash parks, and private beaches for more fun and entertainment. Here are some of the best hotels for families in Turkey:

Haydarpasha Palace: This 5-star hotel in Alanya has its own private beach, 3 children's swimming pools, splash park, water slides, playground, and bowling alley. Parents will love the spa and the all-inclusive option. The hotel has spacious family rooms with 2 bedrooms and 2 bathrooms.

Eftalia Ocean Resort & Spa: This 4-star hotel in Alanya is close to the beach and has a water park, spa, and family-friendly dining. Guests have direct access to Eftalia Island, which is a beachfront entertainment area with swimming pools, splash parks, water park, and play area.

Granada Luxury Belek: This 5-star hotel in Belek has a splash park, play area, fairground rides, spa, and private beach. The hotel has 2 bedroom family rooms with 2 bathrooms. All-inclusive is available. IC Hotel Green Palace: This 5-star hotel in Antalya has a water park, splash park, private beach, spa, and kids club. The hotel has 2 bedroom family rooms with 2 bathrooms. All-inclusive is available.

Apartments And Villas

Apartments and villas are a great option for families who want more space, privacy, and flexibility. You can cook your own meals, do your own laundry, and enjoy the home-like atmosphere. You can also find apartments and villas with shared or private pools, gardens, terraces, and barbecue facilities. Here are some of the best apartments and villas for families in Turkey:

Cappadocia Cave Suites: These cave apartments in Cappadocia are unique and charming. They have fully equipped kitchens, living rooms, fireplaces, jacuzzis, and balconies with views of the fairy chimneys. The property has a restaurant, bar, terrace, garden, playground, and bike rental.

Bodrum Holiday Villas: These villas in Bodrum are modern and spacious. They have fully equipped kitchens, living rooms, dining areas, balconies or terraces with sea views. The property has a shared outdoor pool with sun loungers and umbrellas.

Fethiye Sunset Beach Club: These apartments in Fethiye are cozy and comfortable. They have fully equipped kitchens or kitchenettes, living rooms or sitting areas with sofas or sofa beds. The property has a private beach area with sun loungers and umbrellas.

Side Hill Residence: These apartments in Side are bright and airy. They have fully equipped kitchens or kitchenettes with dining tables or bars. The property has a shared outdoor pool with sun loungers and parasols.

234

Chapter 11 • Travelling on a Budget

Budget-Friendly Accommodation

Turkey is a country that offers a lot of value for money, especially when it comes to accommodation. You can find budget-friendly options that are clean, comfortable, and convenient, without compromising on quality or service. You can choose from hostels, guesthouses, apartments, or hotels that suit your needs and preferences. Below are some of the best budget-friendly accommodation in Turkey that you can check out.

Hostels

Hostels are a great choice for travelers who want to save money and meet other like-minded people. You can find hostels in most of the major cities and tourist destinations in Turkey, with dorms or private rooms, shared or private bathrooms, and common areas such as kitchens, lounges, or terraces. Some hostels also offer free breakfast, Wi-Fi, lockers, and laundry facilities.

Here are some of the best hostels for budget travelers in Turkey:

Cheers Hostel: This hostel in Istanbul is located in the heart of the Old City, within walking distance from the Blue Mosque, Hagia Sophia, Topkapi Palace, and Grand Bazaar. It has a rooftop terrace with stunning views of the city and the Bosphorus. It offers mixed and female-only dorms, as well as private rooms with en-suite bathrooms. It also has a bar, a restaurant, a library, and a 24-hour reception.

Shoestring Cave House: This hostel in Cappadocia is housed in a restored cave house that dates back to the 18th century. It has a garden with fruit trees and hammocks, a terrace with panoramic views of the fairy chimneys, and a cozy lounge with a fireplace. It offers dorms and private rooms with traditional decor and modern amenities. It also has a kitchen, a barbecue area, a laundry room, and a tour desk.

Butterfly Guest House: This hostel in Fethiye is located near the beach and the marina, with easy access to the town center and the bus station. It has a swimming pool with sun loungers and umbrellas, a terrace with sea views, and a bar with live music. It offers dorms and private rooms with air conditioning and balconies. It also has a kitchen, a dining area, a library, and a games room.

Guesthouses

Guesthouses are another option for travelers who want to enjoy a more personal and authentic experience in Turkey. You can find guesthouses in various locations, from urban centers to rural villages, run by local families or individuals who offer hospitality and warmth. You can stay in comfortable rooms with private or shared bathrooms, and enjoy home-cooked meals or local specialties. Some guesthouses also have gardens, terraces, or courtyards where you can relax or socialize. Here are some of the best guesthouses for budget travelers in Turkey:

Sultan's Inn: This guesthouse in Istanbul is located in the historic Sultanahmet district, close to many attractions such as the Blue Mosque, Hagia Sophia, Topkapi Palace, and Basilica Cistern. It has 17 rooms with Ottoman-style decor and modern facilities such as air conditioning, TV, minibar, and Wi-Fi. It also has a rooftop terrace with views of the Marmara Sea and the city skyline.

Goreme Jasmine House: This guesthouse in Cappadocia is located in Goreme village, surrounded by rock formations and valleys. It has 8 rooms with stone walls and wooden floors, equipped with heating, TV, kettle, hairdryer, and Wi-Fi. It also has a garden with flowers and fruit trees, where you can enjoy breakfast or tea.

Dalyan Pension: This guesthouse in Dalyan is located near the riverfront and the town center, with easy access to the beach and the ancient ruins of Kaunos. It has 12 rooms with simple but cozy furnishings, air conditioning, TV, fridge, and Wi-Fi. It also has a swimming pool with sunbeds and parasols.

Cheap Eats and Local Food

Turkey is a paradise for food lovers, as it offers a diverse and delicious cuisine that reflects its rich history and culture. You can find dishes that are influenced by the Mediterranean, Middle Eastern, Central Asian, and Balkan cuisines, as well as regional specialties that showcase the local ingredients and flavors. You don't have to spend a fortune to enjoy the Turkish food, as there are many options for cheap eats and local food that will satisfy your appetite and taste buds. Below are some of the best cheap eats and local food in Turkey that you should try.

Street Food

Street food is a popular and convenient way to enjoy the Turkish food, as you can find vendors and stalls in almost every corner of the city. You can sample a variety of snacks, sandwiches, pastries, desserts, and drinks that are freshly made and served on the spot. Here are some of the best street food in Turkey that you should not miss:

Balık ekmek: This is a fish sandwich that consists of grilled mackerel, raw onion, lettuce, and lemon juice, served in a crusty bread. You can find this sandwich in Eminönü, near the Galata Bridge, where you can enjoy the view of the Bosphorus while eating.

Çiğ köfte: This is a vegan dish that is made of bulgur wheat, tomato paste, spices, herbs, and walnuts, shaped into balls or patties. You can eat them with lettuce leaves, lemon juice, pomegranate molasses, or wrap them in a thin bread called lavaş. You can find this dish in many small shops around the city.

Lahmacun: This is a thin crust pizza that is topped with minced meat, onion, parsley, tomato, and spices. You can eat it plain or with salad, lemon juice, or yogurt.

You can find this dish in many kebab or pide shops around the city.

Kumpir: This is a baked potato that is stuffed with various fillings such as cheese, butter, corn, olives, pickles, sausage, ketchup, mayonnaise, and more. You can customize your own potato according to your preferences. You can find this dish in Ortaköy, near the Bosphorus.

Local Restaurants

Local restaurants are another option for cheap eats and local food in Turkey, as they offer authentic and home-style dishes that are cooked with fresh and seasonal ingredients. You can find local restaurants in different neighborhoods and areas of the city, serving different types of cuisine such as seafood, meat, vegetarian, or regional. Here are some of the best local restaurants for cheap eats and local food in Turkey that you should check out:

Resto Ethnica: This is a seafood restaurant that is located in Karaköy, near the Galata Tower. It offers a variety of dishes such as grilled fish, calamari, shrimp casserole, octopus salad, and more. The restaurant has a cozy and colorful atmosphere with friendly service.

Hidden Garden Restaurant: This is a vegetarian restaurant that is located in Sultanahmet, near the Blue Mosque. It offers a variety of dishes such as lentil soup, stuffed grape leaves, spinach pie, vegetable casserole, and more. The restaurant has a beautiful garden with flowers and trees where you can relax or socialize.

Ziya Baba Turk Mutfagi: This is a meat restaurant that is located in Beyoğlu, near Taksim Square. It offers a variety of dishes such as kebabs, meatballs, chicken wings, lamb chops, and more. The restaurant has a rustic and warm atmosphere with live music.

Goreme Jasmine House: This is a regional restaurant that is located in Cappadocia. It offers dishes from the Anatolian cuisine such as pottery kebab (meat cooked in clay pots), gözleme (stuffed flatbread), mantı (dumplings), and more. The restaurant has a cave-like interior with traditional decor.

Free and Affordable Attractions

Turkey offers a lot of attractions for travelers, from historical and cultural sites to natural and scenic wonders. You don't have to spend a lot of money to enjoy the best of Turkey, as there are many free and affordable attractions that you can visit. Below are some of the best free and affordable attractions in Turkey that you should see.

Istanbul

Istanbul is the largest and most vibrant city in Turkey, and it has plenty of attractions to keep you busy. You can visit some of the iconic landmarks of Istanbul, such as the Blue Mosque, Hagia Sophia, Topkapi Palace, and Basilica Cistern, which are free or have low entrance fees. You can also take a cruise along the Bosphorus Strait, which separates Europe and Asia, and enjoy the scenic views of the city and its surroundings. You can find cheap cruises that start from 15 TL ($1.75) per person. For some fun and education, you can visit the Istanbul Aquarium, which has more than 15,000 marine creatures from different regions of the world, or the Legoland Discovery Centre, which has interactive exhibits and rides for kids. The entrance fees are 120 TL ($14) and 69 TL ($8) per person, respectively.

Cappadocia

Cappadocia is an area of Turkey that is known for its unique landscape, formed by volcanic eruptions and erosion over millions of years. The result is a stunning scenery of fairy chimneys, rock formations, caves, and valleys that look like something out of a fantasy movie. Cappadocia is a great place to go hiking, horseback riding, or biking with your family, as you can explore the natural beauty and discover the ancient churches and villages carved into the rocks. You can find cheap tours that start from 100 TL ($12) per person. The highlight of Cappadocia, however, is the hot air balloon ride that takes you over the surreal landscape at sunrise or sunset. This is an unforgettable experience that will leave you breathless and amazed. You can find cheap balloon rides that start from 500 TL ($58) per person.

Pamukkale

Pamukkale is another natural wonder of Turkey that is worth visiting. Pamukkale means "cotton castle" in Turkish, and it refers to the white terraces of travertine pools that cascade down the hillside. These pools are filled with mineral-rich water that has therapeutic properties and a pleasant temperature. You can swim or soak in these pools with your family and enjoy the relaxing and healing effects. The entrance fee is 80 TL ($9) per person. You can also visit the nearby ancient city of Hierapolis, which was a spa center in Roman times and has ruins of temples, baths, theaters, and tombs. The entrance fee is included in the Pamukkale ticket.

Fethiye

Fethiye is a coastal town in southwestern Turkey that is popular for its beaches, resorts, and water sports. You can find some of the best beaches in Turkey in Fethiye, such as Oludeniz Beach, which has a blue lagoon and a paragliding spot; Calis Beach, which has a long promenade and a sunset view; or Butterfly Valley Beach, which has a secluded cove and a waterfall. You can also enjoy activities like snorkeling, diving, kayaking, sailing, or fishing with your family in Fethiye. You can find cheap tours that start from 50 TL ($6) per person. If you want to explore more of the region's culture and nature, you can visit some of the nearby attractions like Kayakoy Ghost Town, which is an abandoned Greek village; Saklikent Gorge, which is a deep canyon with a river; or Tlos Ancient City, which is one of the oldest settlements in Lycia.

Transportation Tips for Saving Money

Turkey offers many destinations and attractions for travelers. However, getting around Turkey can be expensive if you don't plan ahead and use the right transportation options. Below are some transportation tips for saving money in Turkey that will help you travel more efficiently and affordably.

Fly Or Take The Bus Between Major Cities

If you want to travel between major cities in Turkey, such as Istanbul, Ankara, Izmir, Antalya, or Cappadocia, you have two main options: flying or taking the bus. Flying is faster and more comfortable, but also more expensive and less flexible. Taking the bus is cheaper and more frequent, but also slower and less comfortable. The choice depends on your budget, time, and preference.

If you choose to fly, you should book your tickets in advance and use low-cost airlines such as Pegasus, AnadoluJet, or SunExpress. You should also compare prices on different websites and use money saving sites to look for flight discounts and promotions. You should also be aware of the baggage fees and restrictions of each airline, as they may vary depending on the route and the season.

If you choose to take the bus, you should look for reputable companies such as Metro Turizm, Kamil Koc, or Pamukkale Turizm. You should also book your tickets online or at the bus station to avoid scams or overpricing. You should also check the departure and arrival times and locations of each bus, as they may differ depending on the company and the destination.

Use Public Transport In Cities

If you want to travel within cities in Turkey, you should use public transport instead of taxis or private cars.

Public transport is cheaper, safer, and more convenient than taxis or private cars, as it covers most of the city areas and attractions. You can also avoid traffic jams, parking fees, and scams by using public transport.

Most cities in Turkey have public transport systems that include buses, trams, metros, ferries, funiculars, or cable cars. You can use these modes of transport by buying tickets at kiosks or machines, or by using public transport cards that you can top up and use on different modes of transport. These cards are usually cheaper and more convenient than buying individual tickets.

Some of the public transport cards that you can use in Turkey are:

Istanbulkart: This card can be used on all public transport modes in Istanbul, including buses, trams, metros, ferries, funiculars, cable cars, and suburban trains. You can buy this card at kiosks or machines at major stations or airports for 10 TL ($1.16) and top it up with any amount you want. You can also get discounts for transfers within two hours.

Izmirim Kart: This card can be used on all public transport modes in Izmir, including buses, trams, metros, ferries, suburban trains, and cable cars. You can buy this card at kiosks or machines at major stations or

249

airports for 7 TL ($0.81) and top it up with any amount you want. You can also get discounts for transfers within 90 minutes.

Antalyakart: This card can be used on all public transport modes in Antalya, including buses, trams, metros, suburban trains, and cable cars. You can buy this card at kiosks or machines at major stations or airports for 5 TL ($0.58) and top it up with any amount you want. You can also get discounts for transfers within 60 minutes.

Rent A Car For Rural Areas Or Short Trips

If you want to travel to rural areas or make short trips in Turkey, you may consider renting a car instead of using public transport or taxis. Renting a car can give you more flexibility, convenience, and independence to explore the countryside or visit off-the-beaten-path attractions. However, renting a car can also be expensive if you don't plan ahead and use the right car rental options.

If you choose to rent a car in Turkey, you should book your car in advance and use online comparison websites to find the best deals and prices. You should also use money saving sites to look for car rental discounts and promotions. You should also avoid hiring a car at the airport or from international chains, as they tend to charge higher fees than local companies.

You should also opt for a diesel car instead of a petrol car, as diesel is cheaper and more efficient than petrol in Turkey. You should also check the car condition, mileage, insurance, and fuel policy before signing the contract. You should also return the car with the same amount of fuel as you received it to avoid extra charges.

Chapter 12 • Sustainability and Responsible Travel

Sustainable Tourism in Turkey

Turkey attracts millions of tourists every year with its rich culture, history, and nature. However, tourism also brings challenges such as environmental degradation, cultural erosion, and social inequality. Therefore, it is important to promote sustainable tourism in Turkey, which aims to minimize the negative impacts of tourism and maximize the positive ones for the benefit of the local communities, the environment, and the visitors.

Sustainable tourism in Turkey involves choosing responsible and ethical travel options that respect the natural and cultural heritage of the country, support the local economy and society, and raise awareness about the issues and opportunities of tourism development. Below are some ways to practice sustainable tourism in Turkey:

Choose Eco-Friendly Accommodation

One of the ways to reduce your environmental footprint while traveling in Turkey is to choose eco-friendly accommodation that follows green practices such as energy and water conservation, waste management, recycling, organic farming, and use of renewable sources. You can find eco-friendly accommodation in various locations in Turkey, from urban hotels to rural guesthouses. Some examples are:

Cappadocia Cave Suites: These cave apartments in Cappadocia are unique and charming. They use solar panels for heating and lighting, collect rainwater for irrigation, compost organic waste, and grow their own vegetables and fruits. They also offer eco-friendly activities such as hiking, biking, horse riding, and pottery making.

Bodrum Ecofarm: This farm in Bodrum is a peaceful and relaxing place to stay. It has wooden bungalows with organic cotton bedding, solar water heaters, and compost toilets. It also has a permaculture garden where they grow organic produce and herbs. They also offer yoga classes, cooking workshops, and farm tours.

Hidden Garden Hotel: This hotel in Fethiye is located near the beach and the marina. It has a swimming pool with salt water filtration system, solar panels for electricity and hot water, LED lighting, organic toiletries, and recycled furniture. It also has a garden with flowers and fruit trees.

Support Local Communities And Culture

Another way to practice sustainable tourism in Turkey is to support local communities and culture by choosing authentic and respectful travel experiences that involve interaction with the locals, learning about their traditions and customs, and contributing to their well-being and development. You can support local communities and culture in Turkey by:

Buying local products: You can buy local products such as handicrafts, textiles, ceramics, carpets, jewelry, spices, honey, olive oil, cheese, wine, etc. from local markets or shops that support fair trade and social enterprises. You can also avoid buying products that are made from endangered species or harm the environment.

Eating local food: You can eat local food that is prepared with fresh and seasonal ingredients from local farms or gardens. You can also avoid eating food that is imported or endangered or harm the environment. You can also try some of the regional specialties such as kebabs, pide, gözleme, mantı, baklava, etc.

Participating in local activities: You can participate in local activities that showcase the local culture and heritage such as folk dances, music concerts, festivals, ceremonies, workshops, etc. You can also learn some of the local skills such as pottery making, carpet weaving, cooking, etc.

Protect The Natural Environment

A third way to practice sustainable tourism in Turkey is to protect the natural environment by choosing eco-friendly activities that minimize your impact on the wildlife and ecosystems of the country. You can protect the natural environment in Turkey by:

Visiting natural parks: You can visit some of the natural parks in Turkey that preserve the biodiversity and beauty of the country such as Cappadocia National Park (famous for its fairy chimneys), Pamukkale-Hierapolis National Park (famous for its travertine pools), Kaçkar Mountains National Park (famous for its alpine scenery), etc. You can also follow the park rules such as staying on marked trails, not littering or feeding animals, not picking plants or flowers, etc.

Enjoying nature-based activities: You can enjoy some of the nature-based activities in Turkey that allow you to appreciate the natural wonders of the country such as hiking (e.g., Lycian Way), biking (e.g., Cappadocia), paragliding (e.g., Oludeniz), kayaking (e.g., Kekova), diving (e.g., Kas), etc. You can also choose eco-friendly operators that follow safety and environmental standards and guidelines.

Volunteering for conservation: You can volunteer for some of the conservation projects in Turkey that aim to protect the endangered species and habitats of the country such as sea turtles (e.g., Dalyan), dolphins (e.g.,

Kaş), bears (e.g., Kars), etc. You can also donate to some of the conservation organizations that work in Turkey such as WWF, TEMA, Doga Dernegi, etc.

Eco-Friendly Accommodation and Transportation

If you are looking for eco-friendly accommodation and transportation options in Turkey, you will be glad to know that there are many choices available that will help you reduce your environmental impact and support the local sustainability efforts. Below are some of the best eco-friendly accommodation and transportation options in Turkey that you can consider:

Eco-Friendly Accommodation

One of the ways to find eco-friendly accommodation in Turkey is to look for hotels or resorts that have green certifications or awards, such as the Green Star Certificate, the Green Key Award, or the Travelife Award. These certifications or awards indicate that the accommodation follows green practices such as energy and water conservation, waste management, recycling, organic farming, use of renewable sources, etc. Some examples of eco-friendly accommodation in Turkey are:

Six Senses Kaplankaya: This resort in Bodrum is a luxury eco-retreat that offers wellness and spa services, organic cuisine, and outdoor activities. The resort has a Green Key Award and a Travelife Gold Award for its sustainability practices such as using solar panels, rainwater harvesting, composting, recycling, growing organic produce, supporting local communities, etc.

Hidden Garden Hotel: This hotel in Fethiye is a cozy and relaxing place to stay. It has a Green Star Certificate and a Travelife Gold Award for its sustainability practices such as using solar water heaters, LED lighting, organic toiletries, recycled furniture, etc. It also has a garden with flowers and fruit trees.

Cappadocia Cave Suites: These cave apartments in Cappadocia are unique and charming. They use solar panels for heating and lighting, collect rainwater for irrigation, compost organic waste, and grow their own vegetables and fruits. They also offer eco-friendly activities such as hiking, biking, horse riding, and pottery making.

Eco-Friendly Transportation

A way to find eco-friendly transportation in Turkey is to look for public transport or alternative modes of transport that are low-carbon or low-emission, such as buses, trams, metros, ferries, funiculars, cable cars, bikes, etc. These modes of transport are cheaper, safer, and more convenient than taxis or private cars. You can also avoid traffic jams, parking fees, and scams by using public transport or alternative modes of transport. Some examples of eco-friendly transportation in Turkey are:

Istanbulkart: This card can be used on all public transport modes in Istanbul, including buses, trams, metros, ferries, funiculars, cable cars, and suburban trains. You can buy this card at kiosks or machines at major stations or airports for 10 TL ($1.16) and top it up with any amount you want. You can also get discounts for transfers within two hours.

Electric Buses: These buses are powered by lithium batteries and are quiet and environmentally friendly. They are produced by the Turkish company Aselsan in cooperation with the municipality of Samsun. They can be charged in just 10 minutes and can cover a distance of 90 km on a single charge. They also save fuel and reduce emissions.

Bike Sharing: These are bike rental systems that allow you to rent a bike from one station and return it to another station. You can use these bikes to explore the city or the countryside at your own pace. You can find bike sharing systems in various cities in Turkey such as Istanbul (ISBIKE), Izmir (BISIM), Antalya (ANTBIS), etc.

Ethical Experiences and Wildlife Conservation

Turkey boasts a rich biodiversity and wildlife, with more than 10,000 plant species, 80,000 animal species, and 450 bird species. However, Turkey also faces many threats to its wildlife and habitats, such as habitat loss, fragmentation, degradation, overexploitation, pollution, invasive species, and climate change. Therefore, it is important to support ethical experiences and wildlife conservation in Turkey, which aim to protect and restore the natural environment and its inhabitants, while providing educational and enjoyable opportunities for visitors.

Ethical experiences and wildlife conservation in Turkey involve choosing responsible and respectful travel options that avoid harming or disturbing the wildlife and ecosystems of the country, support the local conservation efforts and initiatives, and raise awareness about the issues and challenges of wildlife protection. Below are some ways to support ethical experiences and wildlife conservation in Turkey:

Visit Wildlife Sanctuaries And Rehabilitation Centers

One of the ways to support ethical experiences and wildlife conservation in Turkey is to visit wildlife sanctuaries and rehabilitation centers that provide refuge and care for injured, orphaned, or confiscated wildlife. These facilities also conduct research, education, and advocacy programs to promote wildlife welfare and conservation. You can visit these facilities to learn more about the wildlife species and their needs, as well as the challenges and solutions for their protection.

Some examples of wildlife sanctuaries and rehabilitation centers in Turkey are:

KuzeyDoga Wildlife Rehabilitation Center: This center in Kars is the first licensed wildlife rehabilitation center in Turkey. It treats and releases injured or sick wild animals such as bears, wolves, lynxes, eagles, owls, etc. It also conducts research on the ecology and behavior of the wildlife species in the region.

DEKAMER Sea Turtle Research Rescue Rehabilitation Center: This center in Dalyan is dedicated to the conservation of sea turtles in Turkey. It rescues and rehabilitates injured or sick sea turtles, especially those affected by fishing nets or boat propellers. It also monitors the nesting beaches and educates the public about sea turtle protection.

Wildlife Rescue Center Izmir: This center in Izmir is run by the Born Free Foundation and the Izmir Nature Conservation Society. It rescues and rehabilitates wild animals such as foxes, jackals, badgers, hedgehogs, etc. It also works with local authorities and communities to prevent illegal wildlife trade and hunting.

Participate In Wildlife Tours And Activities

Another way to support ethical experiences and wildlife conservation in Turkey is to participate in wildlife tours and activities that allow you to observe and appreciate the wildlife and habitats of the country in a responsible and respectful manner. You can participate in these tours and activities by choosing eco-friendly operators that follow safety and environmental standards and guidelines, such as avoiding feeding or touching the animals, keeping a safe distance from them, minimizing noise and disturbance, etc. Some examples of wildlife tours and activities in Turkey are:

Birdwatching Tours: Turkey is a paradise for birdwatchers, as it hosts more than 450 bird species, many of which are endemic or migratory. You can join birdwatching tours that take you to various birding hotspots in Turkey such as Lake Van, Lake Kus, Cenneti (Bird Paradise), Birecik Kelaynak Breeding Station (Bald Ibis), Sultan Marshes National Park (Flamingos), etc.

Dolphin Watching Tours: Turkey has a rich marine life that includes dolphins such as bottlenose dolphins, common dolphins, striped dolphins, etc. You can join dolphin watching tours that take you to various locations where you can see dolphins in their natural habitat such as Kaş (Mediterranean Sea), Foça (Aegean Sea), Istanbul (Bosphorus Strait), etc.

Wildflower Tours: Turkey has a diverse flora that includes more than 10,000 plant species, many of which are endemic or rare. You can join wildflower tours that take you to various locations where you can see beautiful wildflowers in bloom such as Cappadocia (tulips), Antalya (orchids), Artvin (rhododendrons), etc.

Chapter 13 • Language and Culture Quick Reference Guide

Basic Turkish Phrases and Expressions

Learning some basic Turkish phrases and expressions can make your trip to Turkey more enjoyable and rewarding. Not only will you be able to communicate with the locals, but you will also impress them with your interest and respect for their language and culture. Turkish is a fascinating and melodic language that belongs to the Turkic family of languages. It is spoken by about 80 million people, mainly in Turkey, but also in Cyprus, Bulgaria, Greece, and other countries. Turkish is written in the Latin alphabet, but it has some special letters and sounds that you need to learn. Below are some of the basic Turkish phrases and expressions that you can use in various situations:

Greetings And Introductions

The first thing you need to know is how to greet people and introduce yourself in Turkish. Turkish greetings depend on the time of day and the level of formality. Here are some common ways to say hello and goodbye in Turkish:

Merhaba: Hello (mare-aba). This is the most common way to greet someone in Turkish. You can use it at any time of day and with anyone.

Günaydın: Good morning (goon-eye-din). This is a polite way to greet someone in the morning. You can also use it as a farewell when leaving someone in the morning.

İyi günler: Good day (ee-goon-lair). This is a polite way to greet someone during the day. You can also use it as a farewell when leaving someone during the day.

İyi akşamlar: Good evening (ee-ak-shahm-lar). This is a polite way to greet someone in the evening. You can also use it as a farewell when leaving someone in the evening.

İyi geceler: Good night (ee-geh-jeh-lair). This is a polite way to wish someone a good night. You can use it when going to bed or when leaving someone at night.

Selam: Hi (sell-am). This is an informal way to greet someone in Turkish. You can use it with friends, family, or young people.

Hoşçakal: Bye (hosh-cha-kal). This is an informal way to say goodbye in Turkish. You can use it with friends, family, or young people.

After greeting someone, you may want to introduce yourself or ask for their name. Here are some useful phrases for introductions in Turkish:

Adınız nedir?: What's your name? (ah-din-iz neh-deer). This is a formal way to ask for someone's name in Turkish. You can use it with strangers, elders, or superiors.

Adın ne?: What's your name? (ah-din neh). This is an informal way to ask for someone's name in Turkish. You can use it with friends, family, or young people.

Benim adım ...: My name is ... (beh-nim ah-dim ...). This is how you introduce yourself in Turkish. You can use it with anyone.

Tanıştığıma memnun oldum: I'm pleased to meet you (tah-nish-tuh-ma mem-nun ol-dum). This is how you express your pleasure at meeting someone in Turkish. You can use it with anyone.

Basic Questions And Answers

Another thing you need to know is how to ask and answer some basic questions in Turkish. Turkish questions usually start with a question word or end with a question particle. Here are some common question words and particles in Turkish:

Ne?: What? (neh)

Nasıl?: How? (nah-suhl)

Nerede?: Where? (neh-reh-deh)

Kim?: Who? (keem)

Niçin?: Why? (nee-cheen)

Ne zaman?: When? (neh zah-man)

Kaç?: How many? / How much? (kahch)

Hangi?: Which? (han-ghee)

Mı/mi/mu/mü?: Question particle that changes according to the vowel harmony of the sentence.

Here are some common questions and answers that you can use in Turkish:

Nasılsın?: How are you? (nah-suhl-sin). This is an informal way to ask how someone is doing in Turkish. You can use it with friends, family, or young people.

İyiyim, teşekkürler. Sen nasılsın?: I'm fine, thank you. How are you? (ee-yee-yim, teh-sheh-koor-lehr. Sen nah-suhl-sin). This is how you answer the previous question and ask it back in Turkish. You can use it with friends, family, or young people.

Nasılsınız?: How are you? (nah-suhl-sin-iz). This is a formal way to ask how someone is doing in Turkish. You can use it with strangers, elders, or superiors.

İyiyim, teşekkürler. Siz nasılsınız?: I'm fine, thank you. How are you? (ee-yee-yim, teh-sheh-koor-lehr. Siz nah-suhl-sin-iz). This is how you answer the previous question and ask it back in Turkish. You can use it with strangers, elders, or superiors.

Nereden geliyorsun?: Where are you from? (neh-reh-den geh-lee-yor-sun). This is an informal way to ask where someone is from in Turkish. You can use it with friends, family, or young people.

... dan/den geliyorum: I'm from ... (... dahn/dehn geh-lee-yor-um). This is how you answer the previous question in Turkish. You need to change the suffix according to the vowel harmony of the place name. For example: Amerika'dan geliyorum (I'm from America), Almanya'dan geliyorum (I'm from Germany), Türkiye'den geliyorum (I'm from Turkey).

Nereden geliyorsunuz?: Where are you from? (neh-reh-den geh-lee-yor-sun-uz). This is a formal way to ask where someone is from in Turkish. You can use it with strangers, elders, or superiors.

... dan/den geliyorum: I'm from ... (... dahn/dehn geh-lee-yor-um). This is how you answer the previous question in Turkish. You need to change the suffix according to the vowel harmony of the place name. For example: Amerika'dan geliyorum (I'm from America), Almanya'dan geliyorum (I'm from Germany), Türkiye'den geliyorum (I'm from Turkey).

Ne iş yapıyorsun?: What do you do? (neh eesh yah-puh-yor-sun). This is an informal way to ask what someone does for a living in Turkish. You can use it with friends, family, or young people.

Ben ... yım/yim/yum/yüm: I'm a ... (beh-n ... yuhm/yim/yoom/yoom). This is how you answer the previous question in Turkish. You need to change the suffix according to the vowel harmony of the profession name. For example: Ben öğretmenim (I'm a teacher), Ben doktorum (I'm a doctor), Ben öğrenciyim (I'm a student).

Ne iş yapıyorsunuz?: What do you do? (neh eesh yah-puh-yor-sun-uz). This is a formal way to ask what someone does for a living in Turkish. You can use it with strangers, elders, or superiors.

Ben ... yım/yim/yum/yüm: I'm a ... (beh-n ... yuhm/yim/yoom/yoom). This is how you answer the previous question in Turkish. You need to change the suffix according to the vowel harmony of the profession name. For example: Ben öğretmenim (I'm a teacher), Ben doktorum (I'm a doctor), Ben öğrenciyim (I'm a student).

Useful Phrases And Expressions

Finally, here are some useful phrases and expressions that you can use in various situations in Turkish:

Lütfen: Please (loot-fen). This is how you say please in Turkish. You can use it to make polite requests or orders.

Teşekkürler: Thank you (teh-sheh-koor-lehr). This is how you say thank you in Turkish. You can use it to express your gratitude or appreciation.

Rica ederim: You're welcome (ree-jah eh-deh-reem). This is how you say you're welcome in Turkish. You can use it to respond to someone who thanked you.

Afedersiniz: Excuse me / I'm sorry (ah-feh-dehr-seen-ez). This is how you say excuse me or I'm sorry in Turkish. You can use it to get someone's attention, to apologize, or to express regret.

Anlamadım: I don't understand (ahn-lah-mah-dum). This is how you say I don't understand in Turkish. You can use it when you don't comprehend what someone said or wrote.

Tekrar eder misiniz?: Can you repeat that? (teh-krahr eh-dehr mee-see-neez). This is how you ask someone to repeat something in Turkish. You can use it when you didn't hear or understand what someone said.

Türkçe bilmiyorum: I don't speak Turkish (toor-kcheh beel-mee-yor-um). This is how you say I don't speak Turkish in Turkish. You can use it when you want to inform someone that you are not fluent in Turkish.

İngilizce konuşuyor musunuz?: Do you speak English? (een-ghee-leez-cheh koh-noo-shoo-yor moo-sun-uz).

This is how you ask someone if they speak English in Turkish. You can use it when you want to communicate with someone in English.

Yardım edebilir misiniz?: Can you help me? (yah-rdum eh-deh-bee-leer mee-see-neez). This is how you ask someone for help in Turkish. You can use it when you need assistance or guidance from someone.

Oraya nasıl giderim?: How do I get there? (oh-rah-yah nah-suhl gee-deh-reem). This is how you ask for directions in Turkish. You can use it when you want to know how to reach a certain place.

Ne kadar?: How much? (neh kah-dahr). This is how you ask for the price of something in Turkish. You can use it when you want to buy something or pay for a service.

Hesap lütfen: The bill please (heh-sahp loot-fen). This is how you ask for the bill in Turkish. You can use it when you want to pay for your meal or drink at a restaurant or a bar.

Tuvalet nerede?: Where is the toilet? (too-vah-leht neh-reh-deh). This is how you ask for the location of the toilet in Turkish. You can use it when you need to use the restroom.

Sağol: Cheers / Thanks (sah-gohl). This is a versatile word that can mean cheers or thanks in Turkish. You can use it when you want to toast with someone or express your gratitude.

We hope these basic Turkish phrases and expressions will help you have a great time in Turkey.

Turkish Alphabet and Pronunciation Guide

If you want to learn some basic Turkish phrases and expressions, you need to start with the Turkish alphabet and pronunciation. The Turkish alphabet is based on the

Latin alphabet, but it has some special letters and sounds that are different from English. Learning the Turkish alphabet and pronunciation will help you read, write, and speak Turkish correctly and confidently. Below are some of the main features and tips of the Turkish alphabet and pronunciation:

The Turkish Alphabet

The Turkish alphabet has 29 letters, 21 consonants and 8 vowels. There are 23 letters that are similar to the English alphabet, except for Q, W, and X, which are not used in Turkish. There are also 6 letters that are unique to Turkish: Ç, Ğ, I, İ, Ö, Ş, and Ü. Here is the complete list of the Turkish letters and their names:

A a (a)

B b (be)

C c (ce)

Ç ç (çe)

D d (de)

E e (e)

F f (fe)

G g (ge)

Ğ ğ (yumuşak ge)

H h (he)

I ı (ı)

İ i (i)

J j (je)

K k (ke)

L l (le)

M m (me)

N n (ne)

O o (o)

Ö ö (ö)

P p (pe)

R r (re)

S s (se)

Ş ş (şe)

T t (te)

U u (u)

Ü ü (ü)

V v (ve)

Y y (ye)

Z z (ze)

The Turkish Pronunciation

The Turkish pronunciation is mostly phonetic, which means that each letter has a fixed sound and each word is pronounced as it is written. However, there are some exceptions and rules that you need to know. Here are some of the main points of the Turkish pronunciation:

Vowels

The Turkish vowels are divided into two groups: front vowels and back vowels. Front vowels are pronounced with the tongue near the front of the mouth, while back vowels are pronounced with the tongue near the back of the mouth. The front vowels are E, İ, Ö, Ü, and the back vowels are A, I, O, U. Here is how to pronounce each vowel in Turkish:

A a: like the "a" in "father"

E e: like the "e" in "bed"

I ı: like the "e" in "the"

İ i: like the "i" in "sit"

O o: like the "o" in "hot"

Ö ö: like the "u" in "turn"

U u: like the "oo" in "book"

Ü ü: like the "u" in "rude"

Consonants

The Turkish consonants are mostly pronounced like their English counterparts, except for C, Ç, G, Ğ, J, S, Ş, Y. Here is how to pronounce each consonant in Turkish:

B b: like the "b" in "boy"

C c: like the "j" in "jam"

Ç ç: like the "ch" in "chair"

D d: like the "d" in "dog"

F f: like the "f" in "fish"

G g: like the "g" in "go"

Ğ ğ: a soft sound that lengthens or separates the preceding vowel

H h: like the "h" in "hat"

J j: like the "s" in "measure"

K k: like the "k" in "key"

L l: like the "l" in "love"

M m: like the "m" in "man"

N n: like the "n" in "no"

P p: like the "p" in "pen"

R r: a rolled sound like in Spanish or Italian

S s: like the "s" in "sun"

Ş ş: like the "sh" in "sheep"

T t: like the "t" in "top"

V v: like the "v" in "van"

Y y: like the "y" in "yes"

Z z: like the "z" in "zoo"

Vowel Harmony

One of the most important rules of Turkish pronunciation is vowel harmony. Vowel harmony means that words usually have only front vowels or only back vowels. For example, the word "güzel" (beautiful) has only front vowels, while the word "güçlü" (strong) has only back vowels. Vowel harmony also affects the suffixes that are added to words. For example, the plural suffix can be either "-lar" or "-ler", depending on the vowel harmony of the word. For example, "ev" (house) becomes "evler" (houses), while "araba" (car) becomes "arabalar" (cars).

Stress

Another important rule of Turkish pronunciation is stress. Stress means that one syllable of a word is pronounced louder and longer than the others. In Turkish, stress usually falls on the last syllable of a word. For example, in the word "kitap" (book), the stress is on the second syllable: ki-TAP. However, there are some exceptions to this rule, especially for words that are borrowed from other languages. For example, in the word "telefon" (phone), the stress is on the first syllable: TE-le-fon.

We hope this Turkish alphabet and pronunciation guide will help you learn some basic Turkish phrases and expressions.

Cultural Do's and Don'ts

If you are planning to visit this amazing destination, you might want to know some of the dos and don'ts to make your trip more enjoyable and respectful. Below are some tips to help you navigate the Turkish culture and etiquette.

Do dress appropriately. Turkey is a predominantly Muslim country, so it is advisable to dress modestly and avoid revealing clothing. Women should cover their knees and shoulders, especially when visiting mosques or religious sites. Men should also avoid wearing shorts or sleeveless shirts in such places. A headscarf is required for women to enter mosques, so it is a good idea to carry one with you at all times.

Don't diss Atatürk. Atatürk is the founder of modern Turkey and a revered national hero. You will see his portraits and statues everywhere, and insulting him or his legacy is considered highly offensive and even illegal. Respect his memory and avoid any negative comments about him or his policies.

Do learn some Turkish words. Although English is widely spoken in tourist areas and big cities, most Turks are not fluent in it. Learning some basic Turkish words and phrases can help you communicate better and show your interest in their culture. Some useful words to know are:

Merhaba: Hello

Evet: Yes

Hayır: No

Teşekkür ederim: Thank you

Türkçe konuşamıyorum: I don't speak Turkish

Don't get into an argument about football with the locals. Football (or soccer) is a national passion in Turkey, and many people are loyal fans of their favorite teams. However, this also means that rivalries can be intense and heated, especially between the big clubs like

Galatasaray, Fenerbahçe, and Beşiktaş. Avoid getting involved in any debates or disputes about football with the locals, as they might take it personally and get offended.

Do bargain. Bargaining is expected and encouraged at bazaars or markets in Turkey, where the sellers often start with a high price. Don't be afraid to haggle and ask for a lower price, as this is part of the fun and culture of shopping in Turkey. However, be polite and respectful, and don't offer a price that is too low or unrealistic.

Don't buy stones or fossils. Turkey has strict laws regarding the export of antiquities, which include any stones or fossils that might have historical or archaeological value. Buying or selling such items is illegal and can result in fines or imprisonment. If you are offered any stones or fossils by street vendors or shopkeepers, don't buy them and report them to the authorities.

Do visit a Turkish bath. A Turkish bath, or hammam, is a traditional form of bathing and relaxation that dates back to the Ottoman era. It involves soaking in hot water, getting scrubbed by a professional bather, and enjoying a massage. It is a great way to experience the Turkish culture and pamper yourself at the same time.

However, be prepared for some nudity and intimacy, as you will be wearing only a linen towel around your waist.

Do try local food. Turkish cuisine is one of the most diverse and delicious in the world, influenced by various regions, cultures, and histories. Don't miss the chance to try some of the local specialties, such as kebabs, mezes, baklava, kahvaltı (breakfast), çay (tea), kahve (coffee), ayran (yogurt drink), rakı (aniseed liquor), and more. You will be amazed by the variety and quality of food in Turkey.

Don't engage excessively in PDA. Public displays of affection are not very common or acceptable in Turkey, especially in rural areas or conservative places. While holding hands or hugging is fine, kissing or cuddling in public might be seen as rude or disrespectful by some people. Be mindful of your surroundings and limit your PDA to avoid any unwanted attention or trouble.

These are some of the cultural do's and don'ts when visiting Turkey. By following these tips, you will have a more enjoyable and respectful trip to this wonderful country.

286

Conclusion

Turkey is a country that will captivate you with its diversity, beauty, and charm. From the cosmopolitan Istanbul to the ancient Ephesus, from the surreal Cappadocia to the sunny Antalya, Turkey has something for everyone. You can experience the rich culture, history, and cuisine of this unique nation that bridges Europe and Asia, and discover its stunning landscapes, monuments, and beaches. Whether you are looking for adventure, relaxation, or inspiration, Turkey will not disappoint you.

Turkey is also a country that invites you to explore its hidden gems and off-the-beaten-path destinations. You can embark on amazing road trips that will take you to historical and natural wonders, such as the rock-cut churches of Göreme, the thermal springs of Pamukkale, the ancient city of Troy, and the Lycian Way1. You can also enjoy the hospitality and warmth of the Turkish people, who will welcome you with open arms and treat you like family.

Turkey is a country that will leave you with unforgettable memories and a desire to return. Book your trip to Turkey today and get ready for an incredible journey!

Printed in Great Britain
by Amazon